The Greatest Home Based BUSINESS in the World

> **Learning to say,
> "I did it my way."**

Written by
Randy Joe Ward

COPYRIGHT 1996
by
Randy Joe Ward

MEMBER
NATIONAL
SPEAKERS
ASSOCIATION

"All rights reserved. No part of this
book may be reproduced in any form or
by any means without the prior written
permission of the COPYRIGHT OWNER."

FIRST PRINTING ...... MARCH 1996

PRINTED IN THE UNITED STATES OF AMERICA

Published by
Making a Difference Seminars
333 American Way
Jennings, OK 74038
(918) 757-2235

Dedicated to

my children

**Randy Joe Ward, II
Cherami Chantel Ward
Jeremy Kalon Ward**

and
my grandchildren

**Dakota Delane Ward
Randi Rachelle Ward**

PREFACE

Even though this book is directed to the entrepreneur, the powerful principles and concepts apply to all areas of life. No matter what you do for a living, reading this book will enhance your ability to create and maintain empowering relationships and attract whatever your heart desires. It will inspire you and enhance your ability to produce results.

Throughout this book, when I use the masculine pronouns he and him, I mean the feminine as well. This book was written for all men and women who want to be the best that they can be.

CONTENTS:

Part One: Setting the Stage

Chapter One:
> **In Search of the Ideal Business ... 13**

Chapter Two:
> **Free Enterprise ... 23**

Part Two: The Performance

Chapter Three:
> **The Game of Survival ... 33**

Chapter Four:
> **The Accelerated Game of Life ... 39**

Chapter Five:
> **The Winner's Way ... 41**

Chapter Six:
> **What do You Really Want? ... 45**

Chapter Seven:
> **Normal Game vs. Accelerated Game ... 51**

Chapter Eight:
> **Learning the Value of the Products ... 61**

Chapter Nine:
> **Structuring and Commitment ... 67**

Chapter Ten:
> **The Principles of Accelerated Winning ... 73**

Chapter Eleven:
> **Daring to Dream Again ... 93**

Chapter Twelve:
> **A Player's Natural Progression ... 107**

Chapter Thirteen:
> **Establishing a Game Plan ... 121**

Chapter Fourteen:
> **Getting the Ball Rolling ... 135**

Chapter Fifteen:
> **The Bimonthly Forum ... 139**

Chapter Sixteen:
> **The Monthly Forum ... 153**

Chapter Seventeen:
> **Conclusion ... 163**

Part Three: Epilogue

Chapter Eighteen:
> **Starting Your Own Business ... 169**

Chapter Nineteen:
> **Business Ownership ... 177**

Part One...
Setting the Stage

In this section, you'll learn some advantages of a home based business that you haven't even thought about.

If you've lost your passion for business, this fresh new look just might restore it!

CHAPTER ONE...

IN SEARCH OF THE IDEAL BUSINESS

If you've been in business for years, it's only natural to have discovered what aspects of business ownership work for you. But perhaps you have never owned a business and don't have a feel for the associated problems.

In order to understand the problems, all you need to do is question the people you know who own businesses. In doing so, you will get responses similar to those that follow. They are the answers given to us by persons to whom we asked, **"If you were to create for yourself an ideal business, what would one of** its most important features be?"

HOME BASED

Wayne Raleigh is a master plumber. With tools in hand, he is poetry in motion. Wayne can get more work done in a day than most three men. He's a valuable tradesman and earns a good living.

Wayne's ideal business is one which is "home based." You see, Wayne lives fifty miles west of Tulsa, Oklahoma and has to drive an hour to work each day. He thinks it would be great to not have to fight traffic - to be able to wake up in the morning, walk downstairs, and be at work.

LOW CAPITAL REQUIREMENT

David Frick has done quite well in the metal fabrication business. His company, DAVCO, builds equipment for the oil industry, such as: oil tanks, gas separators, heater-treaters, pump jacks, etc.

David's ideal business is one which requires only a small amount of capital to start up or expand. His current business required hundreds of thousands of dollars worth of equipment to start, and for years now, all of his profit has gone toward the purchase of additional equipment. He says, "There seems to be no end in sight."

NO ACCOUNTS RECEIVABLE

In recent years, Lester Sparks has built a frac tank service to serve the oil industry. After accumulating thousands of dollars worth of accounts receivables, and loosing lots of sleep, he decided to sell out.

Currently, he considers that an ideal business would operate on a cash basis, eliminating the temptation for clients lacking integrity to take advantage of him.

NO EMPLOYEES

With 17 convenience stores, Terry Duff is continually hiring, firing, replacing and rescheduling employees. His ideal business is one that includes people as partners, but not as employees.

NO INVENTORY

Sam Gertner, owner of Agape Auto Repair, has a business consisting of body shop, transmission shop and general auto repair. He stocks thousands of dollars worth of parts and supplies.

With so much at the risk of fire or casualty, Sam can't afford to leave his inventory uninsured. Even so, his sleepless nights are the result of another problem, theft by employees.

Sam envisions an ideal business which requires no stocking of inventory.

FREEDOM

Bill Moore has a thriving printing business and has done our printing for years. Personally, if it weren't for Bill, we would use a more convenient shop. Evidently, a lot of his customers think likewise, because every time he has let someone else manage the business, it has gone downhill. It is critical for Bill to be there during normal working hours, and his ideal business would offer more freedom and flexibility.

Instead of being run by his business, he would like to run it for a change. He would like to work when he wants to work, and not work when he doesn't want to work.

NO TERRITORIAL LIMITATIONS

It's shocking to learn about the "red tape" involved in getting a permit to operate a small trucking business.

After months of "politicing" and deals, Jerry McCutchen, finally got a permit to haul oilfield equipment. Since crossing the state line requires Interstate Commerce Commission permits, he was confined to one state.

Jerry's ideal business has no territorial limitations, the opportunity to work wherever he happens to be.

TAX ADVANTAGES

Dana Ham, and his wife, Jan, travel a lot and feel that an ideal business would be such an integral part of their life that virtually all expenses would be business related, and therefore tax-deductible. Their ideal business would provide them with lots of what they love, "tax deductions."

UNLIMITED POTENTIAL

Doctor David Pillow is an emergency room physician whose income is great, but directly proportional to the number of hours he works. This situation places

In Search of the Ideal Business

a ceiling on his income. He can't duplicate his earning power as a doctor, so his ideal business would of-

fer unlimited potential, and not be dependent on the small number of hours which are available for personally produced results.

LOW OVERHEAD

Jay Anthony is a dynamic young man who owns a chain of tanning salons. Each link in his chain has a monthly overhead exceeding $2,000. His income is very seasonal, and, during the off months, his overhead remains the same. Time and time again, Jay has seen businesses crippled and closed by high overhead, coupled with low cash-flow. He says, "The higher your overhead, the more 'in the hole' you are before you start. You have to produce a lot of business every month just to break even. This kind of pressure tends to devastate your peace-of-mind."

Jay's ideal business would not require a fixed overhead or be susceptible to cash-flow problems.

The Greatest Home Based Business in the World

LOW RISK

The owner of Think Snow, Rick Biggert, recently decided that the ideal business would contain little or no risk.

In order to earn a high rate of interest on his company's working capital, he placed it into an uninsured Savings and Loan Association. Rick never considered there to be a risk, yet the S & L is now bankrupt and his money is gone.

CHALLENGE AND DEVELOPMENT

Tulsa Tops is a company which manufactures formica cabinet tops. Its owner, Jeff Ward, has found that the business no longer offers a challenge, and that there exists very little opportunity for personal growth. His ideal business would offer the endless variety and challenge of people, as well as, the opportunity to fully develop the potential of being human.

FAMILY PARTICIPATION

Ken Roland has spent years "on the road" selling family portraits. Since his photography business has cost him many hours of being with his family, Ken's ideal business is one in which his family could participate.

TRAVEL AND CONTACTS

Dan Gaddy believes, "It's not what you know, but who you know." His beauty supply business limits his contacts to a small geographic area and to a certain type. Dan's ideal business would enable him to travel and meet people on a national and international scale.

EXCITING, FUN AND FULFILLING

David Chancellor says, "I've been in a rut all too often. My ideal business is one that's exciting, entertaining, fun, and fulfilling."

PART-TIME

For Shelby Oakley, an ideal business is one which generates a passive income that can be maintained on a part-time basis. Currently, his fence company, Aaron Fence, requires that he work, what seems to be, all the time. He wants more leisure time to pursue hobbies and recreation with his family; the time to express those interests which don't manifest a lot of money.

ON THE JOB TRAINING

Randall Thomas considers the opportunity to earn while he learns to be an important feature of an ideal business.

A SUPPORT SYSTEM

Paul Kleb's ideal business has a built-in support system. He says that no one begins life as an experienced business person. Since business skills must be learned, he wants a cooperative partnership with people who know business, and who are willing to teach him in such a way that he can in turn teach others.

GOOD PRODUCTS

Tony Thomas is self-employed as a manufacturer's rep. In his earlier days, several of the products he distributed lacked the quality which he now demands. His ideal business involves a high-quality product that is priced fairly, that meets a need and is backed by a 100% money-back guarantee.

UNCOMPROMISING INTEGRITY

Richard Imprescia, a minister considers uncompromising integrity to be a feature of his ideal business. He wants to be able to close his eyes with all the money on the table and know that it will remain there. No one would ever loose money in his ideal business.

OPPORTUNITY TO CONTRIBUTE

How about Randy Ward? As the owner of a variety of businesses, past and present, I have come to realize that virtually any business can serve as a vehicle to contribute to others. My ideal business is a network of people-serving-people.

If the above features exist, your business is one in which your partners and customers will enjoy an enhanced sense of aliveness. So, let's review and list the characteristics of an ideal business:

1. Home Based
2. Low Capital Requirement
3. No Accounts Receivable
4. No Employees

5. Little or no Inventory
6. Freedom
7. No Territorial Limits
8. Tax Advantages
9. Unlimited Potential
10. Low Overhead
11. Low Risk
12. Personal Challenge
13. Family Participation
14. Travel & Contacts
15. Exciting & Fulfilling
16. Part-time
17. On the Job Training
18. A Support System
19. Good Products and/or Services
20. Uncompromising Integrity
21. Contribution

No matter how much time you spend analyzing different types of businesses, you are going to be "hard pressed" to find one that incorporates these ideals as well as a home based direct selling business. For many, direct selling is the only game in town.

By designing your own business around these principles, you will create a vehicle that will carry you and your associates to the destinations of your wildest dreams.

The search is over!

The Greatest Home Based Business in the World

Your thoughts determine what you want. Your action determines what you get. Only action produces results.

Randy Ward

CHAPTER TWO...

FREE ENTERPRISE

Somewhere along the way, in the last 220 + years, we lost sight of what free enterprise could be here in America. There was a time when each person owned his or her own business, or at least had a very open invitation to own such a business.

Now, only a small percentage of the population owns a business. The social environment no longer supports the idea. Instead, it supports the idea of having a "good job" and working for someone else. To me, there is no such thing as a "good job".

To many, the word JOB is an acronym for "Just

The Greatest Home Based Business in the World

Over Broke". For me, it's an acronym for "Jumping Over Bumps". The first of the month comes along, and you get a paycheck that enables you to jump over the bump known as a mortgage or rent payment. Then, the middle of the month comes along, and you get another paycheck that enables you to jump over the bump known as a car payment, etc. This vicious circle continues month-after-month, and you spend your entire life "Jumping Over Bumps"!

People carry on about how poor people should want to work, as if working for someone else is a great joy in life. At the same time, the opportunity for a poor person to create his own business has been absent for so long that entire generations of people have come and gone, and what it can mean to own one's own business has been forgotten.

I must admit, it's tempting to try and find a villain who is responsible for this tragedy. The great department store founders, the magnates of the automobile industry, great oil tycoons, and all of the employers of the top corporations could be indicted. In a way, all of these are pyramid schemes, with one person sitting on top of a rigid pyramid structure, with the masses working in the middle of the pyramid, in positions from which it is very difficult to move up.

It is unlikely that anyone is going to start as a janitor for one of Detroit's giant automobile makers and end up as the president. I am not saying it can't be done. I am saying that the environment does not support it happening.

Free Enterprise

There is not a free enterprise system but, rather, a slave or pyramid enterprise system. People are

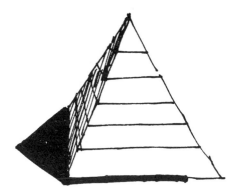

not motivated. The incentive is not there. There is no experience of owning the corporation.

If you work for a corporation for fifteen years, for example, you build tremendous value into it, and that value persists for many years. Suppose you decide to leave! How much of that value do you take with you? Suppose you are incapacitated and can't work anymore. How much of the value, which you built into the corporation, do you take with you? **NONE,** that's how much.

DIRECT SELLING / NETWORKING TRANSFORMS THE MARKETING WORLD!

Old habits are truly hard to break. Even bad habits, bad attitudes, and false beliefs are difficult to give up. Many people are close-minded to direct selling because it requires one to develop new business standards.

The Greatest Home Based Business in the World

The old, accepted way of conducting business is no longer appropriate, for a person who is committed to transformation. Only those persons, who can throw out the old models of how business operates, can understand how direct selling shifts business from competition, opposition, and a win/lose situation, to cooperation, empowerment and a win/win situation.

The accepted way of making money is unconscious, un-examined, and un-transformed. It is an environment where "real success is only for the lucky or for those who inherit it; where they get there by cheating and taking advantage of others; or where success is not available to the ordinary person, etc."

Since most people think this way, it's no wonder so few become successful. The American job ethic states that you should help someone else make their dreams come true, by working for them for 40 to 45 years, and then retire on a pension amounting to one-half of the income on which you were already broke. Working for someone else is usually a win/lose situation - the employer wins while the employee looses.

TYPICAL BUSINESS

Typical business is un-transformed in that most participants have their experience of value in life diminished by it. No wonder 36 out of every 100 men die from stress related illness before reaching the retirement age of 65. No wonder only 5% of our population are financially independent by age 65, and most of them are the employers. Another 5% are so broke at age 65 that they can't retire, and 54% retire on a subsistence income. These statistics are sad, but true.

We must realize that we have been brainwashed. Society is structured to keep us from experiencing our potential. Many people, who work "by the hour," are motivated to be inefficient, and far too many people are motivated by welfare, to not work at all.

You may even be in a job that produces money for you as a function of "your ability to not get the job done quickly"!

Most employees can't wait for 5 PM or the weekend. They live to get off work because they sense the lack of integrity in their workplace. They know that they are killing themselves by drawing a salary in a win/lose game, and they can't wait until 5 PM, Friday, and age 65.

"I QUIT"

More and more people are developing the courage to stand up and say, "I quit! No longer will I make money in this way." Their approach to business is fresh and creative. They realize that the old models no longer work - that they destroy aliveness and potential.

A truly transformed business is a "you and me" business, where I can win only if you win, and where I can experience your success as my own.

As a player in the old business game, you receive an average profit, of, let's say, 30% to 40%, for personally producing a service, or the sale of a product. In the new business game, you're not only a personally producing player, but a coach as well. Since this new game rewards your personal production, and your coaching ability through several generations of players, the percentage is split so that a portion of it can be paid on each level. The better you coach, the better results your players will produce, and the greater their income and yours.

Instead of being rewarded for not getting the job done quickly, the new game rewards us in direct proportion to our effort and ability. It enables us to experience a true sense of accomplishment and satisfaction. The old way of doing business leaves people crippled. It stifles their creativity, their energy, their desire, their dreams.

A WIN/WIN BUSINESS

Most people are so convinced that real success is for someone else that it is, in fact, for someone else. But an ideal business, a transformed win/win business, allows one to transcend the old ways of thinking. For those of you who are aware enough to live transformed lives, direct sales is a great way to earn a living. **It's the best game in town.**

Owning your own home based direct selling business allows you to dream, to have an exciting purpose, and to contribute greatly to others. It enhances the experience of life and self, for all who participate. In a direct sales business, we work hard assisting others to be successful in their own businesses. We train them, step-by-step, until they know their business in such a way that they can go train others. Our job becomes that of a coach who loves and serves his, or her, trainees.

FROM A JOB TO A GAME

Direct Sales shifts earning a living from a job to a game. It is a proven way to turn your dreams into reality, by helping others turn their dreams into reality, a true win/win situation. Your dreams can all come true if:

1. YOU DARE TO HAVE DREAMS.
2. YOU GET OUT AND DO SOMETHING.

Society is full of people with a lot of talent who haven't been as successful as they could be, simply because they haven't found the proper vehicle. Direct Sales and/or Networking can be that vehicle.

WHAT IS A NETWORK?

A network is a group of aligned people who are in communication with each other. For your network to succeed and sustain, it must contain the following elements:

1. a common purpose,
2. duplication,
3. a commitment to the success of others, and
4. open lines of communication.

For the next couple of weeks, jog your memory with the following statement:

**THE MOST POWERFUL WAY FOR
ME TO MAKE A DIFFERENCE,
WHILE EARNING A LIVING,
IS NETWORKING!**

Be grateful for who you are and what you have, right now, and it can only get better.

Randy Ward

Part Two... The Performance

In 1984, my first edition of ***Winning the Greatest Game of All*** was published. Thankfully, the book became one of the best recruiting, training and motivational tools available in the world of home based direct selling. Now in its sixth printing, leaders in the industry have purchased copies by the box-full to present to members of their organizations, in a wide variety of companies. The reason is that these hard hitting principles really work, usually, even in spite of a lack of support by uplines or the companies involved.

Here, in Part Two of this book, you will see the powerful philosophies from ***Winning the Greatest Game of All*** come to life in the lives of our main characters, George and Shirley Seeker.

In the search for a quality life, why is WINNING the shortest path to success? We have all heard the expression that "we learn more from our failures than we do from our successes." Unfortunately, for most of us that has been true. I say unfortunately because what we learn from our mistakes is usually far less life-giving than what we learn from our successes. Our errors teach us to be cautious, fearful and hesitant, but doing something right, which I call WINNING, teaches us to be confident, courageous and determined to continue winning in even greater ways.

I have often thought, wouldn't it be great if a company came into existence that patterned its entire operations, including compensation plan, training and motivation upon these winning principles.

You were probably given this book so that you could better understand the magic and power of operating your own home based business. You will find that the rules are clear and duplicatable, and a step-by-step game plan is provided. It clarifies what you are up against, what is required and the potential rewards. After reading this book, you will be able to make a quality decision as to whether you want to be a participant or spectator, whether you want to play or sit on the side lines.

I assure you, it's much more exciting and fulfilling to play the game than to merely watch it. After all, most people fail at business and the "game of life" because they are not even in the game. This book will have a tendency to throw you in the ring with the confidence and equipment necessary to become a champion.

I have chosen the story form as the simplest way to introduce you to the most workable and practical system of individual empowerment that I have ever experienced. These rules of success are not new. They are drawn from many sources. What is new is a structured use of the principles, which greatly augment their power. In this story, we are able to follow our venturers, George and Shirley Seeker, as they discover a way to accelerate themselves toward a more successful life.

This story is for those who want to be great WINNERS. I hope you enjoy using what you learn. As a result, you and the people you bring into this powerful experience will enjoy healthier, happier and more productive lives.

Randy Joe Ward

CHAPTER THREE...

THE GAME OF SURVIVAL

George Seeker was thirty eight and had done rather well for himself in the fifteen years since graduating from college. His insatiable desire to learn, to be and to have, had enabled him to be coached by some very capable teachers. He had found that the more willing a person is to be coached, the quicker and easier he or she will achieve success. During that time, he had been coached to success in the businesses of insurance and real estate, as well as, land development, construction and oil. But after learning the rules of each particular business, formulating a game plan and being coached to success, he found the excitement and feeling of fulfillment would be gone. So he would then repeat the process in a different business venture.

Actually, the "Game of Survival" and the "Money Game" were extremely challenging until he became financially independent via real estate development at the age of thirty-six. By then he was searching for a new challenge, a new meaning. The financial security met a need, but he found that real happiness, peace-of-mind and inner satisfaction were still missing. Of course he had heard that money can't buy happiness, but suddenly he found himself confronted with that harsh reality. He was faced with the fact that all of us have a deep-rooted, burning desire to believe our lives make a difference. We all want to know that we have lived and played the game so that we have made a CONTRIBUTION to life.

Even though he rather unconsciously knew

The Game of Survival

that the desire to contribute is basic to our natures, it had not been a driving force in his life -- as long as he was playing the Survival Game. So after getting SURVIVAL handled, his insatiable drive began to focus on a desire to "save the world," so to speak.

Consequently, he was often confronted with desires like:

• trying to have greater peace of mind and assisting others in experiencing the same.

• seeking empowering relationships with family and friends and empowering others to do likewise.

• being loved unconditionally and being able to love others in that capacity.

• being accepted the way he was and returning the same consideration.

• having the freedom to do what he wanted to do and enhancing the freedom of others.

• being a "high-performance" person with a spark which motivates others.

• maintaining good health and being an example for others.

• experiencing his own empowerment and

inspiring others to experience their own.
- and so forth.

For the first time in his life, George found himself not really going anywhere. Then the seemingly impossible happened. The world fell in on him. With the collapse of the real estate market, his leveraged position wiped out his equities. He was not only broke but deeply in debt. Bankruptcy looked like a real necessity, but he was determined to hold on and eventually pay off all his creditors, 100% on the dollar.

As he made one arrangement after another, his creditors were impressed with his determination, but doubtful that he could pull it off. With a depressed economy in that part of the country, there were few options.

George found a job in an Insurance company where he was soon promoted to assistant department manager, making $46,000 a year. Up to then, his wife, Shirley, had stayed home raising their three kids, but had now gone to work making $1,300 a month.

With the payments on the debt and the escalating costs of the family, there usually wasn't enough money to reach the end of the month. George was desperately looking for ways to supplement his income. He had thought of going back into real estate, but with the state of the economy, he knew his income would get smaller before it would get larger. He had to keep his job, limiting as it was.

Then a friend, John Recruiter, brought him a ray of hope.

The Greatest Home Based Business in the World

If you are not willing to risk the unusual, you will have to settle for the ordinary.

Jim Rohn

CHAPTER FOUR...

THE ACCELERATED GAME OF LIFE
"Buying into the Sizzle"

John Recruiter had recently joined a popular multilevel marketing company. The concept of network or multilevel marketing (MLM) was not new to George and his wife, Shirley. They had been invited to attend introductory meetings for a number of marketing opportunities and had even gone to a few, but up until now they had never gotten involved. But when John began telling them about his company, with its rapid growth and some of the incredible commission checks being received, George began to pay attention, especially when he heard that some ordinary people were making over $20,000 a month.

The idea of having an income from his own part-time business made some real sense to George. The products, which were selling like hotcakes, sounded interesting, too. With George's background, it looked like he could easily duplicate what the big hitters were doing. John Recruiter kept reminding him how great it would be to be his own boss again, use his communicative skills and not only get out of debt, but become financially independent. Then John showed George how, with a little investment of several thousand dollars in a start-up inventory, he could move instantly all the way up to the group leader level and receive the maximum commissions.

So for the first time, George took the MLM challenge. He found a way to put up the money and started contacting friends. He used the same "bait" of talking about big checks, great products and financial independence. With his credibility and enthusiasm, he enticed quite a few to join with a similar investment.

His second month's check was over ten thousand dollars, and things looked great. But he found that his friends were having less success than he and were sorry they had listened to him. That began to bother George and he found it harder and harder to assure his other friends how easy it was supposed to be.

Finally, he unhappily accepted the fact that the program was not working out for most of those in it. Even though he still had a substantial inventory of product in his garage, he stopped contacting more friends. George vehemently concluded that this was not only his first time to try MLM, but it was going to be his last. He would just have to find another way to make extra money to pay off his debts. George could not remember a time in his life when things looked so hopeless. He even found himself yelling at the kids more often and arguing with Shirley over even little things. Life just wasn't much fun anymore.

CHAPTER FIVE...

THE WINNER'S WAY

Nearly six months later, something began happening at the office which caught George's attention. He began noticing a young woman in his data entry group, a previously reserved and shy person named Irene Chin. George noticed a dramatic change in her aliveness. She had suddenly blossomed. Her Productivity was up and so were her spirits.

"You're certainly a cheerful breeze of sunshine these days," George commented while passing her in the hall.

With a big smile and twinkle in her eyes, she chuckled, "Yes, Mr. Seeker, I'm a Winner!"

Surprised that he had not heard about her winning some big prize, he asked, "What prize did you win?"

"Oh, no. I haven't won any prizes. What I mean is that I used to concentrate on how not to be a loser. But a month ago my husband and I were invited to join a group that supports its members in 'making the most out of life'. It works because we help each other develop the attitudes and habits which cause life to work and be more rewarding. There are products that have enhanced our lives and enabled us to create a residual income.

"It really is working, Mr. Seeker. It's also helping at home with my family and it is helping here at work. It is incredible."

George had never heard so many words come out of this previously bashful young lady. He thanked her politely and moved on, but he could not help marveling and wondering what her new project was all about. It sounded like a church or self improvement group, but her talk about products and residual income ruled that out.

Several days later, he could not restrain his curiosity any longer and asked her for some literature on "that program she was in." Her answer surprised him again.

"I have some materials but I would rather have you meet a person we call The Winner. He sponsored the person who sponsored me."

"No, that's okay Irene," George quickly responded. "Just give me some of their literature. I would like to read up on it first."

Irene got a little mischievous glint in her eyes and laughingly replied, "The company has a whole manual, but that isn't what it's all about. Just reading about it first might throw you off track, and I don't want to do that to you, Mr. Seeker. I respect you too much. What you need to do is talk with The Winner. I am sure that he would love to answer all of your questions. I think he still has some time available tomorrow night."

George had some other plans, so he started to decline. Then he paused to reconsider. Irene's friend, The Winner, might be the one he needed to talk to if he was going to get his life back on track. He decided to change his schedule and agreed to take the first available opening. Later, Irene Chin gave him a note:

The Winner has reserved thirty minutes tomorrow, Tuesday at 8:45 PM.

He is anxious to meet the Great George Seeker.

Address: **654 Orchard Lane**
Phone: **789-3546**

Irene Chin

To be reborn is a constantly recurring human need.

Henry Hewes

CHAPTER SIX...

WHAT DO YOU REALLY WANT?

George Seeker had timed his drive so that he was ringing the doorbell at 8:44 PM. For some strange reason, there seemed to be an inner excitement about this meeting. He wondered why he wanted to make a good impression by being exactly on time. After all, The Winner would be trying to sell him on his program, what ever it was, not the other way around.

The attractive woman who met him at the door introduced herself as Jean, The Winner's wife. Her gracious, truly warm greeting made him feel very much appreciated and somewhat special. The Winner came out of his study with a departing guest. Introductions were exchanged and George was invited into the den. The whole house was tastefully furnished, but the den was George's idea of what he had planned before the bottom had dropped out of his world.

"I really appreciate your being willing to meet at

this late hour, George," The Winner began. "We have a remarkable program and I'm scheduling around the clock, two days a week."

"Sounds like my doctor's hours," George responded.

"Well, the rest of the time, Jean and I fly to places around the country. We have friends all over and we don't want to leave them out. Irene tells me some very good things about you, George. She says you are one of the best people she has ever worked for. At the same time, I realize you are here because you are looking for an opportunity to better yourself. Is that right?"

"Well, you know how it is with a family," George smilingly, but cautiously, answered.

"You bet. Most people could use more income and we have an answer for that. But, believe it or not, the way we are structuring our program, the money, and it can be substantial, comes almost as a by product. Our real reward is an enhancement and transformation of ourselves toward a more fulfilling life.

"You have heard the saying, 'Most people are so busy making a living they never get time to make a life.' So before we start, I could use some help, George. Would you share with me where you are, right now, with your life and career?"

For the next five minutes, while The Winner listened intently and occasionally asked more specific questions, George found himself revealing things that he had hardly admitted to himself. He told of his drive to be very successful financially and the lack of real contentment and satisfaction in the process. George

What do You Really Want?

was a little surprised to hear himself describe the time before the crash when he thought that, if he could help change the world, he might finally fill that inner void. But because of bad economic conditions, he had taken a beating and was back on the treadmill. Yes, he did have a good job, but he was more of a paper shuffler than a creative administrator. He worked long hours but was making very slow headway.

The Winner finally asked, "Of all the things in the world you could do to make a living, what would you like to be doing more than any other?"

George looked blank for a moment, then said, slowly, "Boy, that is kind of hard to say. But come to think of it, if I could make enough money at it, I would like to be teaching."

"Teaching what and where?" The Winner inquired.

Hesitating a moment to be sure he wanted to reveal one of his deepest fantasies, he said, with a big grin, "You know what I have always wanted to do is to teach leadership and management. I have been in a number of those courses, and I don't know when I have enjoyed myself more."

The Winner let out a laugh of delight, slapping his guest's knee and exclaiming, "That is exactly what I had always wanted to do, too! George, you are going to love what you're getting yourself into!"

"Okay, what in the world am I getting into?"

"Well," The Winner answered, "it is something we call the Accelerated Game of Life.

"Life is like a great party, put on for us by a very wonderful Host at his great estate, called Earth. The entertainment at the party is called the 'game of life' where we fulfill our inherent needs for comfort, attention, recognition, love and usefulness. But most of us feel that we don't get to play the 'game of life' enough because we are stuck with the Survival Game and the Money Game. Although these are aspects of the 'game of life,' most of our friends have become slaves to them, without the freedom to play the big game."

George, nodding his head in agreement, asked, "So you are saying that there is an Accelerated Game of Life?"

"Yes, the 'normal game of life' is the path of least resistance. What we have is not for everyone, because many shy away from the demands of rapid personal empowerment and a more direct path to expanded friendships and greater independence, wealth, travel and making a difference. We create the opportunity through the vehicle of sharing products and values."

George answered, "If by that you mean MLM, I have heard the pitch and even tried it about a year ago. I have decided that it is not for me."

The Winner smiled broadly. "Sounds like my story. Let me tell you what got me involved. Up until a year ago, I had a very profitable law practice, helping people get at other people or protecting them from someone who was trying to get at them. In my early years, it was fun beating the pants off of 'the enemy' but in later years, it was getting to be more like a rat-race than real fun. Then a year ago, at the age of 42, I met a man who hit me with two simple questions:

What do you really want to be doing with your life? Why aren't you doing it?

"Those questions hit me in the face like a '2 by 4'. In fact, they forced me to look at my life objectively. I discovered, similar to what you have found, what I enjoyed most were those times when I was teaching some of my distraught clients how to become more fulfilled and happier with their lives.

"Once I became clear on what it was I really wanted, I was shown how I could start part-time, immediately, and get paid for it while I was mastering the new skills. In addition, because of combining greater self-actualization with the dynamics of a simple business of sharing values, I saw that, in five years, I could build up a greater residual income than I could normally expect to do in my practice in the next twenty. That got my attention. It was the beginning of an entirely new direction for my life. It wasn't that I was learning anything I didn't already know, but I had forgotten most of it.

George, what has been changing my life since then is a process which got me doing what I already knew I should be doing and wasn't. My life has been more fulfilling and satisfying than I had dreamed possible."

George, still wondering where all this was going, asked a little doubtfully, "Are you saying that you think you found a way to change the world after all?"

The Winner laughed heartily again, fascinated with George's blunt appraisal. "No, George, the first step is to accept the fact that the world isn't going to be saved by either of us, all by ourselves, and even if we could, it wouldn't be our responsibility. Our main responsibility, as a teammate in the game of life, is to play full-out and promote teamwork. Coming to grips with the fact that we are all teammates and all have important positions to play, it becomes clear that anytime we make a positive difference in an individual's life, it affects the entire team. In other words, we can make a difference in the world by helping one person.

It became clear that fulfillment can only come from the experience of life itself! The game of life is where we fulfill our inherent needs of acceptance, love, relationships, health, freedom and really making a difference.

"Even though the Survival Game and Money Game are aspects of the 'game of life,' most of our teammates are slaves to them just like we were, without the freedom to play the big game. It's sort of like wanting to play Major League baseball and being only old enough to play Little League. So when my friend asked me what I really wanted to do in life, and why wasn't I doing it, I felt that I had NO CHOICE!"

"Like a good coach, he said to me, 'But wait, my friend! There just might be a choice! Wouldn't it be great if you could start sharing the Accelerated Game of Life and get paid for it? Wouldn't it be great to earn while you learn? Wouldn't it be great to discover such an accelerated course in the fulfillment of life?'"

CHAPTER SEVEN...

NORMAL GAME versus
ACCELERATED GAME

The Winner paused and took a deep, satisfying breath and leaned forward with a bigger smile than usual. "George, the normal game of life is where the majority of our teammates are, and it is merely the path of least resistance. The game contains most of the elements -- such as, relationships, personal growth, the money game, the opportunity to make a difference, etc. But the Accelerated Game provides the opportunity to develop our skills more quickly. It is a way to speed up the process of personal growth, a much more direct path to friends, wealth, travel and making a difference.

"My friend assured me that the Accelerated Game of Life is not for everyone. It is hardball, and he contended that many people have failed at it because they never knew the rules. **They tried to play hardball with softball rules.** No wonder so many people experience frustration.

He told me that he was not interested in leading sheep to the slaughter - that his intention was to provide me with what is needed to play and win. He said that he wanted me to enter the Accelerated Game of Life, knowing what I was up against, knowing the rules and having a step-by-step proven game plan.

"So George, like my coach did for me, I must talk straight to you, telling it like it is! You must know what you are up against, what the rules are and the potential rewards. Only then can you make a quality decision to play or watch. As a hardball coach, we cannot spend time with those who want to play softball. No matter how skilled we are, and no matter how well-coached, we cannot win the accelerated game playing by the normal rules."

George wasn't sure he understood what The Winner was getting to, but he liked the direction it was going, so he asked, "What is the Accelerated Game of Life?"

"The Accelerated Game is a vehicle through which we can fulfill our needs more quickly. The vehicle is any business or project which involves such elements as recruiting, hiring, training, acknowledging, motivating, empowering, managing and developing people. This could be any type of public service which requires self-expression and maintaining empowering relationships with others.

"Actually, there are several vehicles which can accelerate you out of the rut of the normal game of life. One of the best vehicles is owning your own business, but not just any business. It must be one which provides a quality product or service, and one through which you can contribute to others. Another vehicle is the popular, but misunderstood, business of network marketing."

"Yes," George interrupted. "As I mentioned, I got burned about a year ago, when I gave such a company a try. It was a very discouraging experience."

The Winner paused, letting the smile drop from his face. "Actually, network marketing has the potential of providing an excellent opportunity for average people to accelerate themselves toward the best which life has to offer. But as an infant in the field of marketing, this form of opportunity has experienced a lot of mischief, giving it a negative image. What many people don't realize is that, in most cases, it was front-end loading 'pyramid schemes' and 'chain letters' which created the mischief. At present, network marketing is entering into a more mature phase. But even then, most of the money goes up to the high producers so that the rest of the people can't make enough money to stay in the game."

George asked, doubtfully, "Is there any way to make the networking business really fair so that everybody wins?"

"Oh yes, but I have a little surprise for you. You

The Greatest Home Based Business in the World

came here tonight expecting me to pitch you on my business, right?" The Winner smilingly inquired.

George grinned right back, "Of course, aren't you?"

The Winner replied, "No, not tonight. I am going to let my friends do that for you at another time. Our real purpose tonight is for you to find out what we mean by the Accelerated Game of Life and greater empowerment.

"I want to know whether you are interested in playing such a game full-out! As I said, 'This isn't for everyone.' You can't play the game of hardball using softball rules."

"Well," George Seeker interrupted. "I can tell you for sure you have got my attention!

The Winner picked up a large art pad and a marker. At the top he printed the word, WINNING, then underneath, GETTING WHAT YOU REALLY WANT.

"When we say we want to be a success," The Winner began, "the term means different things to different individuals because we put priorities on different desires. I like to divide our desires into two main categories."

He printed on the board, with spaces in between, the following headings:

WINNING
Getting what you really want!

| SURVIVAL | CONTRIBUTION |

Normal Game vs. Accelerated Game

The Winner, directing the thoughts of his guest, said, "George, I want you to think of what you would need in order to feel that you have been totally successful in the area of SURVIVAL!"

George hesitated, then said, "The most obvious is to be out of debt, have financial independence again, be able to travel, have free time and be able to afford the good life."

"Yes, very good and another one," The Winner added, "is good health, isn't it? The fact is that the healthier and more responsive we are, the better our performance will be. As they say, health is wealth."

George added, "Yes, and to feel totally successful, I would need to be the BOSS, the one who has the flexibility of options and who gets to choose. Do you think that is an important element?"

The Winner definitely agreed and finished writing the four points under the first heading:

SURVIVAL:
   A. Financial independence
   B. Freedom of time
   C. Vital health
   D. Being in charge

At this point, The Winner took a deep breath, smiled broadly, and declared, "Now we come to the most important desire of all, CONTRIBUTION. Every one of us has a deep yearning to make a difference, to have our life mean something! Like when you saw that SURVIVAL was not enough, that is when you thought you would have to try to change the world.

"We get a satisfying feeling by making a Contribution. Yet most people are so stuck in Survival that they never really discover the transforming empowerment of making Contribution a first priority.

"But contribute what? Contribution means assisting others in fulfilling their desires of survival, achievement, recognition and contribution. Like the old saying, the way to get what you want is to help others get what they want. So here they are:

CONTRIBUTION:
   A. To the survival of others.
   B. To the achievement of others.
   C. To the recognition of others.
   D. To the contribution of others.

"I have dealt with our two basic desires of Survival and Contribution in this detail," The Winner continued, "because it helps most of us see what has kept our lives from unfolding to their full potential. As children, we automatically started at the Survival level and gradually discovered other levels of desire. What we need to see is that most of us have been concentrating so much on our own Survival needs that the other desires have dwindled in power and satisfaction. The disadvantage of this is that Survival perpetuates itself. Because we get caught up in Survival, we never seem to have enough, no matter how much we have. As both of us found, it is a jealous master."

George Seeker had a smile back on his face as he spoke, "I can see that we want success in all of our

Normal Game vs. Accelerated Game

desires, but because we are so heavily involved in the need to WIN in Survival, we fall short in the big WINS of life. Between my wife and myself, we have take-home pay of nearly $50,000 a year, but it is far from enough."

"That was my story too," The Winner continued. "Now we are ready to identify the central key to what we are doing. Something incredible happens when our order of emphasis is reversed. When we come first and foremost from Contribution, then our financial needs seem to be met automatically."

"Absolutely. I have always believed that, even though I haven't done it," George answered.

"Through Contribution we find ourselves achieving more and more, which takes the impossible demands out of our Survival needs. What I am talking about helping you create, George, is much more than a business. It is the Accelerated Game of Life. In it we utilize the process of building and managing an organization, but we come from Contribution rather than Survival. Does this make any sense to you?"

"I love it," the guest said with conviction. "This is certainly a different way to approach network marketing than anything I have ever seen before."

"Yes, since most people in networking are coming from Survival, that is how they pitch it. They draw the circles and multiply the percentages, talk about huge incomes, free time, more friends, self-development and the works. If the pitch is done well, people can get very excited and motivated. However, since most people cannot mass-recruit or do volume sales, they soon get disillusioned and have to be replaced."

George responded, "I have been doing a lot of soul-searching while we have been talking. I am a little shocked at how complacent I have been during my business career. I guess I assumed that there is no way to change the direction I developed as an attitude of life. I had just inwardly believed that some great and glorious day I would arrive, and I would have everything and live happily ever after. But that is just fantasy. So what is the next step? What enabled you to change the direction of your life?"

"The business vehicle we use to play the Accelerated Game of Life is Network Marketing, and the founders of our company have created a Compensation Plan that is as unique as their emphasis on Contribution rather than Survival.

Most Distributors find the marketing plan easy to work because it is built around the POWER OF THREE. You sponsor and work with only three key players at a time. As our Associates do this, the growth continues to be very significant. We call the overrides we receive residual income because, like dividends on stock, the revenue does not require that you work for it every day. George, does this sound interesting enough for you to want to look into it further?"

George liked The Winner. There was no doubt that he came from the heart and his own experience of both a transformation in his life and an ability to make enough money to leave his law practice. With no

Normal Game vs. Accelerated Game

hesitation, he made a big grin and replied, "You bet! I want to know more."

"Are you free tomorrow morning for breakfast?" The Winner asked with an exaggerated sober look.

"Tomorrow? What time?"

"Seven o'clock at the Coffee Shop on South Main and Tenth. One of our Associates, John Davis, is meeting with a few of the people with whom I met today. He will explain our products and services and how the bonuses are earned."

As the two men stood up, George Seeker reached out his hand for a very firm handshake and said, "Now I know why you are called The Winner. I could call Irene a Winner, too. I can't get over how she has changed. She is really fantastic. I have her to thank for getting me here tonight, and you to thank for getting me to thinking like a Winner again."

The Winner gave him a firm embrace and then said, "George, I want to acknowledge you for the great contribution you have made to me by spending this half hour with me tonight. I am truly impressed with your willingness to see what you really want."

As the two men walked out into the hall, a young couple was waiting with Jean. Their appointment was at 9:15 PM and George noticed that the time was exactly that.

After introductions and a warm farewell, George stepped out into the dark, cool night. "Wow!" he mused to himself. "I like it! Just wait until Shirley hears about this."

The Greatest Home Based Business in the World

Happiness is the light on the water. The water is cold and dark and deep.

William Maxwell

CHAPTER EIGHT...

LEARNING THE VALUE
OF THE PRODUCTS

George Seeker did not sleep much that night. He had so many thoughts to share with his wife, Shirley. Ideas kept turning in his head about the new direction their lives could take. She was thrilled to see him so enthused about something. That had not happened for a long time. Because of the children and her job, she could not make the morning meeting, but George assured her that he would give a complete report.

The Coffee Shop had an excellent breakfast buffet. John Davis and his group of eight guests were starting their meal in a small, private dining room when Davis, a congenial man of fifty-two, with a friendly, relaxed smile, started the session. He had already gained the group's respect as a gracious host who was excited about being able to contribute another step in their new adventure. As the guests had arrived, he had seen that each became acquainted and felt comfortable.

John commenced by telling his own story. He said, "A little over six months ago, I was introduced to The Winner by a friend of mine. Isn't that an incredible experience?"

"He's quite an amazing person," Cora, an older woman in the group, commented.

George Seeker laughingly added, "He shook up my complacency all right!"

John continued, I went to my introductory meeting just to do a friend a favor and was confident that I would find plenty of reasons for not being interested. I am a high school teacher, though not for long now, I want you to know. I have taught for twenty years and was content to be in a fairly comfortable rut. The only thing I was sure of was that no one was going to get me into sales or marketing. Yes, I still needed more income, but I was not about to go in the hole with a shaky chance of striking it rich. But even more important, I was, in a sense, emotionally and spiritually flat. Now don't get me wrong. I was an active participant in my church. I thought of myself as a true believer. Yet my spiritual life was in a humdrum, 'so what' mode. Even worse, I didn't even notice it, even though my lack of joy and love showed up at home with my family. It

Learning the Value of the Products

effected my teaching, too.

"But those were not the reasons I became a distributor. I joined because I saw a chance to get more bang for my buck, so to speak. When I saw what the products and services could do for my family and understood the power of duplication, I could not afford to say no.

"First, then, is to answer your questions about our company. How are we different from other programs?"

John drew three interlocking circles on the board. In the first, he wrote **Unique Products** and went on to explain the company's products and services.

Next, John wrote **Distributor Services** in the second circle and explained the company's state-of-the-art order processing, voice mail, teleconferencing, fax-on-demand and other support systems.

"As you will find, our company is built on the **Power of Three.** Not only do we have Unique Products and Distributor Services, we have something just as important as either of these. We have **Distributor Training,**" which he wrote in the third circle.

"We're not just looking for Distributors, but people who want to *Make the Most Out of life.* The company is continually training its Distributors in the different ways to use the products and services and even helps motivate them to do so.

"Have any of you had a chance to go through the list of products yet?" Several raised their hands, but the rest were like George, anxious to have a look. John loaned each a Product Brochure. As they briefly went through the products, John gave a description of each, and the group began to share real excitement.

George Seeker was impressed. Sam, a well-built man in a business suit, asked, "What does it cost for a Distributorship?"

John laughed, "I thought you would never ask. Actually, it was my next point." He then explained the low initial cost and added, "Remember, our company is not just interested in bodies. We want people who are committed to becoming the best that they can be.

"The real reason behind the formation of this company was not just to provide great products. Neither was it just to give us a chance to earn some residual income, although I want to tell you that, already, after just six months, I am halfway to matching my income as a teacher."

In a brief description, which took less than five minutes, John reviewed the lucrative compensation program built on the power of three. Then he emphasized, "The main purpose of this company is to make a real difference in our lives. The founders knew from their own experience that most of us change very slowly when we try to do it on our own. So they looked for a business which would be a vehicle where those involved could play a game called, *'Let's Make the Most Out of Life.'*

"The first part of that game I have given you this morning, which is to improve your quality of life and standard of living.

"We also have dynamic training for our Associates

Learning the Value of the Products

on how to build their own business. That business is NOT about selling or getting other people to sell. We are not in sales, in the normal sense of the word. Nor is it about SURVIVAL. We are into sharing information. That is really all we have to do because, as you can see, the products are so unique and the distributorship is so valuable that they actually sell themselves.

"Our business training has to do with how you invite your friends into a way of coming from CONTRIBUTION as a team player in the Accelerated Game of Life. It is enabling people like ourselves to discover that their natural state is that of being a Winner."

At this point, John paused for what seemed like a very long time, but probably no more than a quarter of a minute. Then, with a little strain as he held back some emotion, he spoke slowly and said, "My friends, I do not believe there is any way you can understand this morning what is going to happen to your lives. I certainly had no idea six months ago, but I want you to take my word for it, we are not kidding when we say you are going to experience a growth in all the things you treasure most, such as your depth of love and appreciation for being alive. You are going to treasure your loved ones even more, and that includes the rapidly expanding group of people you become associated with in this business.

"You are going to be empowered through growing in trust and being trusted. You will understand integrity in greater depth. You are going to begin being enthusiastic much more of the time. You are going to grow in your willingness to acknowledge those around you for being the WINNERS that they are."

John Davis concluded by saying, "I will now pass out some company literature. I want to acknowledge you for coming here so early and on such short notice. It indicates some very strong determination to enhance the quality of your lives. You have certainly been a thrilling reminder to me of how great all of us are."

John finished by instructing the members of the group to get in touch with the person who had invited them. George Seeker stayed briefly to clarify some points with John and then went off to work in a very happy but thoughtful mood.

CHAPTER NINE...

STRUCTURING AND COMMITMENT

By the time George Seeker got to work that morning, he could hardly wait to tell Irene about his impressive experiences of the previous twelve hours.

"I was sure you would like our WINNING PROGRAM. I have your New Distributor Kit back at my desk," Irene answered with delight. "I'll meet you in the cafeteria during lunch and explain it to you."

George was a little late getting to the cafeteria, but quickly sat down with his tray next to Irene. She had the kit opened and the Application set in place. He completed the form by electing to have the fee for the kit and a standing monthly product order to be applied against his credit card. As he skimmed through the Product Catalog, he began shaking his head in amazement, and half mused out loud, "These people really mean what they say about quality and value!"

With one of her biggest smiles, Irene reached into the kit and took out an audio cassette tape. "Mr. Seeker, this tape is so important that I am going to ask you to make me a promise."

"What kind of a promise," George responded with a serious voice to mimic her emphasis.

"Are you and your wife going to be home tonight?" she asked. George nodded his head. "Then what I want you to promise me is that both of you will listen to this tape tonight. It will explain the products and services in detail, along with testimonials."

George willingly agreed. Then, placing the audio tape back in the box, he asked, "What's our next step, Irene?"

Answering with a playful giggle, Irene said, "The most important meeting is yet to come. You have been shown only two of the ten principles of our *Accelerated Game of Life.* The Winner showed you how we can come from the principle of CONTRIBUTION instead of SURVIVAL. This morning, John Davis showed you how our company demonstrates the principal of TRUE VALUE through its Unique Products and Distributor Services."

George replied, shaking his head, "Irene, I had no idea anyone had taken this approach. This thing is win, win all the way through."

Structuring and Commitment

"Yes," she agreed. "The next two principles are built into our compensation plan. They are the principles of STRUCTURING and COMMITMENT."

"I can understand Commitment, but what do you mean by Structuring, Irene?"

"As an Associate, we want you to accept the responsibility for sharing the value of this outstanding business opportunity with a minimum of three of the best people you know. Our program is structured around the POWER OF THREE. Two is too few, four might be too many to start out with.

"To help you fulfill your responsibility to support them, we recommend that you initially sponsor only three committed 'key players' on the first-level of your Primary Team. These three become your key executives, like vice-presidents, in building your own organization. In turn, we want you to give these three friends your full commitment to help them find their three."

Then Irene drew another level to the TRIPLEX.

George saw the value of the TRIPLEX structuring and commented, "I like it! I have already got several people in mind."

Irene nodded her head, understandingly. "Our first commitment to you, Mr. Seeker, is to help you get your first three people. When your three people get their three, you will have nine on your second-level. When those nine get their three, you will have twenty-seven on your third-level."

The Greatest Home Based Business in the World

She completes the third level and writes:

A Qualified Team, which makes you a Team Manager.

"At this point, you have thirty-nine people in your organization and we call you a Team Manager.

"My husband and I would be so delighted to have you as one of our first-level key players, but we already have our three. Consequently, we have been thinking about who should be your sponsor. One of our first-level Distributors is Harold Johnson. He does printing for my husband. Harold is just getting started, and we would like for the two of you to meet. I think you would work great together. My husband and I, along with Harold and his wife, are available tomorrow night to come over for a visit. Is there anything you and your wife can't set aside tomorrow evening?"

"I'll check with Shirley," George answered, hopefully. "Is this just for getting acquainted?"

"No," she said with emphasis, "it is a lot more than that. In fact, this is the most critical meeting we will have together, because we want to see if our program is a workable vehicle for you to fulfill your dreams. It usually takes us most of the evening. Of the three aspects to our program, we feel this is the most crucial area of all."

Irene picks up another napkin and draws three interlocking circles.

In the first she writes **Quality Products** and in the second, **Residual Income.**

Before she fills in the third, she says, "This third

Structuring and Commitment

one is the most important part of all. It is really the fundamental reason the founders created our company." Then she writes **Individual Empowerment.**

"So tomorrow night," she continues, "the first item of business will be to review the **Ten Accelerated Principles of Empowerment.** My husband, Lee, will lead that discussion. It scared him the first time he did it, but he really loves it now. He is becoming a wonderful teacher. After that, we will help you set up your **Game Plan.** Believe me, you will love it!"

George was sure that he would. That evening he enjoyed rehearsing the morning events with Shirley. Then they listened to the cassette tape. The message was like a travelogue, taking them on a journey through the Products and Services. They frequently stopped the tape in order to discuss the items that interested them most.

Also, they jotted down questions about some of the products. As both lists grew longer and longer, they became more and more impressed. This was exciting and they found themselves wondering about the meeting the following evening.

As they finished the tape, George noticed a little inner voice of self-congratulation telling him that he would be able to report to Irene Chin that his commitment to hear the tape had been accomplished. He smiled at his anticipation of her happy acknowledgment.

Yes, this was fun.

The greatest truths are the simplest, and so are the greatest men.

J. C. and A. W. Hare

CHAPTER TEN...

**THE PRINCIPLES OF
   ACCELERATED WINNING**

The next evening, Irene and Lee Chin arrived with Harold and Claudia Johnson, a handsome couple in their early thirties. As they all enjoyed some of Shirley's light refreshments, Lee asked the Johnsons to give a brief account of their background and why they had decided to join the company. Then Irene shared her story, followed by her husband's.

As each spoke frankly of their up's and down's in their search for high-level survival and greater fulfillment, a warm empathy filled the room. The Seekers were impressed and felt honored to have such "real" people in their home. George was openly surprised to

The Greatest Home Based Business in the World

learn the background and achievements of his previously shy, data entry operator.

Then Lee Chin continued, "I want to thank each of you for sharing. George and Shirley, we want to get better acquainted with you, too, as you have with us, and we will do that when we work with you later tonight on your Game Plan and the steps for fulfilling your goals. Will that be all right?"

As George nodded approval, a little thrill of excitement went up his back, bringing a slight flush to his face, which he tried to cover with his famous grin.

"The Ten Accelerated Principles of Winning," Lee said as he held up a flip chart, "have to do with a well proven approach to self-empowerment and a quality life." Lee turned the first page of the flip chart over and the word <u>Scientific</u> was printed vertically.

```
S
C
I
E
N
T
I
F
I
C
```

"Shirley, when you hear this word, SCIENTIFIC, what comes to your mind?"

Shirley thought for a moment and then said, "I

think of Scientific as being objective, methodical, accurate, precise and very SCIENTIFIC." She laughed at using the world to define itself.

"Very good," Lee acknowledged. "So if we can enhance our lives in a more Scientific way, we would have a much greater chance than if we just flew by the seat of our pants, going hit or miss.

You notice that the word has 10 letters, and each letter stands for an essential principal of Accelerated Winning. The first letter in SCIENTIFIC is S, which stands for the most effective means of achieving change, the STRUCTURING PRINCIPLE.

1. STRUCTURING

To make change a necessity.

"It is said that 'necessity is the mother of invention.' We might also say, necessity is the mother of change. So if I desire change, the wisest thing to do is create the NECESSITY FOR CHANGE. Do you all agree that we tend to do what we HAVE TO DO?"

At first, Shirley objected, insisting that she did many things she didn't have to do. But through the brief discussion, she began to see that the pressure of increased necessity usually changes a "want to" into a "got to".

Lee continued, "So if I realize this key to self motivation and really want to form a new habit, I will have a better chance of success if I set up some requirements where I have to do it. Have any of you set yourself up like that?"

The Greatest Home Based Business in the World

Claudia Johnson responded, "Yes, I buy expensive vitamins, and I used to forget to take them. So when I purchased some several months ago, I made a deal with my kids that if they caught me at mealtime taking my first bite of food without having my vitamins, the one catching me got a quarter. Boy, is it working. In fact, I find it so easy for me to remember that sometimes I pretend to forget so I can reward their diligent policing."

Lee, with a chuckle, thanked her for sharing and said, "Can any of you recall where our company structures performance in the Compensation Plan?"

George gave the example Irene had taught him about encouraging Associates to sponsor only three 'key players' at a time, so that they will focus their support on helping those three become qualified.

"Exactly, George," Lee responded. "That STRUCTURING is making a world of difference in our program. And you notice that the requirements are easy enough so that we do not eliminate the vast majority of people who could only bring in a few."

2. COMMITMENT
To choose to get a job done.

Lee Chin turned the flip chart. "The second letter in SCIENTIFIC is C which stands for COMMITMENT.

Nothing happens in our life without commitment. Even to stand up requires a commitment, a definite decision, an actual choice. Great achievements require great commitments.

"What we teach each other in our program is how to decide what we need to do to reach a goal and then create the necessity to do those things. Claudia, I heard that you discovered a way to get yourself to stay in contact with your new Associates. Share that with us, will you?"

Claudia Johnson, making a big, bright-eyed grin, began, "Since the most critical time for a new Associate is their first few weeks, we should contact them every day for awhile. A week ago we sponsored our first person.

"I told her that I would call her every day for the next two weeks and asked if she would appreciate that? She was delighted, so I took my next step. I 'structured necessity' for myself by getting her agreement that for any day that I did not call, I was to pay her $10. It is fantastic. In the past I have made promises for daily follow-up, but after a few days, I would go hit or miss. Wow! This way it is so easy to remember. We really make a game out of it. She says when I call, 'Oh heck. You just cost me $10.' The best part is that I feel so good about keeping my commitment."

Lee enthusiastically added, "What a terrific way to combine commitment to structuring, Claudia. I'm impressed. That is the way we can make our major commitments for long range goals work, by identifying the essential components for reaching the goal and then creating the 'necessity' for performing those components."

Lee turned the next page of the flip chart. "The

third letter is I for INDIVIDUAL EMPOWERMENT."

3. EMPOWERMENT
To keep my word.

Lee turned to George and asked, "How would you describe a person who you feel is empowered?"

George answered, "Obviously, he would be very honest and trustworthy."

"Absolutely," Lee agreed. "He would have real INTEGRITY. Trust and empowerment go together. It is said that a person is only as powerful as he keeps his word. Unfortunately, it has become very common for people to feel that a promise is binding only if they do not have an excuse for not fulfilling it. Excuses are a substitute for integrity. The fact that people do not keep their agreements is the most basic reason why their lives are not working, meaning that their lives are not truly satisfying.

"Claudia's COMMITMENT to call her new Associate every day has INTEGRITY. She is keeping her agreement. Her friend is learning that Claudia means what she says, that she can be trusted to accomplish what she has promised - a call or $10, right?

"You see folks, everyone has some integrity. Everyone can be trusted to some degree. But that is the problem, to some degree, because most people function with only relative integrity. When we choose a standard of ABSOLUTE INTEGRITY, an incredible thing happens in our lives, relationships, families and businesses."

The Principles of Accelerated Winning

Shirley interrupted with a question, "But what about 'the best laid plans of mice and men?' How can anyone keep every commitment?"

"That is an excellent question," Lee responded. "My wife has had quite an experience with that. Would you share your experience Irene?"

Irene was delighted to respond. "Since becoming more conscious of what I promise, I have been much more realistic about what I say I will do. The other day The Winner asked me to meet him at a certain time. I told him I would try, and he reminded me that a promise to try amounts to no promise at all. I told him of the other things that I had to do and that they might take longer than expected, so how could I make an agreement to meet him at that specific time?

"The Winner asked me, 'If your daughter was on the verge of dying and I had the medicine which could save her life, would you be there on time?' I told him, 'Of course. I would take my daughter, go there right now and sleep on your doorstep, if there were any question about being able to get what I needed to save her life.' Instantly I saw what he meant. It is not a matter of IF and TRY, it is a matter of choice as to priorities."

"Thank you Irene," Lee acknowledged. "So we become more conscious of where our commitments lie. Most people are committed to things of relative inconsequence. In our program, we are committing to a more empowered way of life."

Then George Seeker inquired, "But, as Shirley

asked, what about those times when things don't work out?"

Lee answered, "Simple! We clean up the mess as fast and as adequately as we can. We communicate, accept responsibility for having broken our agreement, then do whatever can be done to go on from there."

Harold Johnson spoke up, "For example, in my printing business, if I tell someone a job is going to be done by a certain time and I have failed to take into account that my ability to perform was contingent upon a doubtful shipment of paper arriving on time, and the paper does not arrive, I am fully responsible for the broken agreement, and I will clearly acknowledge it and do what I can to 'clean up' the mess. The fact that I was sincere in my promise is immaterial. The truth is I used poor judgment. I misled them to expect something that I did not produce. Sure, I will tell them the story, but not to get me off the hook. After all, I have to admit to myself that if my life had depended upon it, I would have had that job done, one way or another."

"Okay," George added, "I know what you mean. It's amazing how much easier things work out when I don't get off on the 'don't blame me' kick and just admit my responsibility and do what I need to do to make it right."

Lee continued, picking up the pace, "Individual empowerment means that 'we walk the talk'. We demonstrate what we teach. For example, if we are excited about our products and find new, creative ways to use them, so will our organization! If we are going to play the sharing game, we play full-out, which means setting the pace. It means, as well, training and motivating our teams to be successful in the business opportunities. So, individual empowerment means:

..to develop our communicative skills.

..to develop our leadership skills.

..to operate our own business.

..to supplement our income.

..to be the best we can be.

..to become financially independent.

..to play life full-out.

"Personal empowerment means becoming, doing, and having just about anything in life. Why? Because empowerment is LIFE - The Accelerated Game of Life."

Lee continued, "It is said that growing in enlightenment is becoming LIGHTER by discovering that life is a wonderful game. We can accelerate enlightenment by discovering that we can be playful much more of the time - at home as well as at work - that the most natural state for us to be, is PLAYFUL."

Lee picked up the flip chart again, turning the page, and saying, "Our fourth letter is E which stands for ENTHUSIASM."

4. ENTHUSIASM
To be playful.

Lee Chin paused before going on. "This one was the hardest for me because I have always tried to hold my emotions inside. But when I was reminded that the word ENTHUSIASM comes from 'In Theo' -- meaning God Within -- something inside of me clicked.

"Enthusiasm is easy to experience when everything is going well, like when we have friends boosting us, when we are making lots of money, when no one ever crosses us at home, and when we are 'high' in spirit. But to have enthusiasm all of the time, twenty-four hours a day, I knew that was something else. If we want to accomplish a lot, have more friends, have people want to be around us, love us, admire us -- then we want to unleash our natural state of enthusiasm. Why? Because enthusiasm is an irresistible force! It attracts!

"Down deep, everyone wants enthusiasm. We can enjoy the roller-coaster of life by getting to know a thrilling, strong, playful, magnificent person - ourselves."

Lee was speaking faster and louder. His enthusiasm was contagious, filling the room with energy. He was allowing himself to get carried away -- much to the delight of Irene, whose head was bobbing up and down as high as her smile was wide.

"You know," he confided, "I had become a master at holding back my own playfulness. In the last month, I have been practicing not holding back. I no longer wait for special occasions. If we are enthusiastic all the time, then every day is a special day, and it becomes a special day for everyone we meet. Irene and I are even getting out of bed enthusiastically."

Claudia joined in, "We have all heard that it is a fundamental law of psychology - 'Act the part and you will become the part'. I have been consciously practicing enthusiasm all week and it is making a wonderful difference."

5. NOURISHING
To acknowledge everyone's WINS.

Lee thanked her, and as he turned the flip chart, said, "Yes, one of the most powerful ways to express our enthusiasm for life is to acknowledge others. We all want to be acknowledged. It is like psychological nourishment. If we are to accelerate the game of WINNING, we must increase the recognition and approval we give to others. **Enthusiasm is the way we play. Nourishing is what makes it play.**"

Harold Johnson motioned for a chance to speak. "George and Shirley, my new approach to working with people in my printing plant is to *catch them doing something right.* That was a big switch for me. I was always trying to catch them doing something wrong, so I could help them improve. It has really surprised me to find that people do a lot better by learning from their hits, than they do from their misses."

Lee continued, "Thanks, Harold. We all know the importance of nourishing others with compliments, but we so frequently forget. So, during my Forum Meeting last week (that's when I meet with my first-level Team), we set up a structure for praising. Claudia, since you were there, would you share with the Seekers what we did?"

Claudia began, "Harold and I realized that we needed to build a stronger habit of praising people, so we made up a contest to see who could give the most compliments to different people in the next twenty-four hours. Each of us had a little bag of beans. We took a bean out each time we gave a person a compliment. I couldn't believe how much more fun it made everything -- at work, out shopping, getting the car fixed, seeing the neighbors, being with the family. My score was one hundred and six, and I WON! At the Chin's next Forum with us, I will get five minutes of group praise as my prize. In fact, Lee is threatening to get me a big button that says I LOVE NOTICING."

The room exploded with laughter and a little ribbing about her implied new button.

Then Lee continued. "The first five principles, Structuring, Commitment, Individual Empowerment, Enthusiasm and Nourishing, have special emphasis on how we relate to others. The next four have to do with how we take care of ourselves, because WINNING is both an inside and an outside job. I am going to cover them only briefly because we deal with them in much greater depth in our Forum Program." A new page of the flip chart was turned.

6. TRUE VALUE

Giving and receiving value.

Lee continued, "The TRUE VALUE PRINCIPLE means that we judge our activities to see if we are giving or receiving TRUE VALUE. As that principle

The Principles of Accelerated Winning

applies to our company, it means that we commit to using our products to the maximum and teaching our people, not only to do the same, but to teach and motivate their people. It means learning how to use the products and benefits by listening to the audio and/or video tapes, and attending trainings."

"Mr. Seeker," Irene broke in, still not wanting to call her boss by his first name, "that is why I made you commit to listening to the tape that was in your starter kit. Did you like it?"

"Yes, Irene, but since we are going to be in your team, please call me George." Irene smiled modestly and nodded her head. "Actually, I appreciated your emphasis on listening to the tape the very first night. We both have not only gained a greater appreciation for the products, but we did exactly what you said. Shirley, show them our lists."

The group was both pleased and impressed, commenting on how much product knowledge the Seekers had already acquired. Then Lee turned to number seven on the flip chart.

7. IMAGINATION
To see goals vividly.

"By IMAGINATION, we are referring to our ability to create an enhanced inner image, or picture, which can reprogram our subconscious and erase the inferiority conditioning all of us carry over from our past. Some marvelously simple, extremely effective methods, using positive affirmations, which we feel and visualize, create the positive habitual attitude essential for real satisfaction and happiness.

"Historically, one of the most effective ways of reprogramming the subconscious has been through affirmations. However, unless affirmations are done correctly and consistently, they will not work very well. As conscious WINNERS, we can enhance the words of the affirmations with feelings and visualizations. The resulting impact is absolutely miraculous. When you come to defining your agreements with the Johnsons, they will go over what we call our Positive Expressions."

As Lee turned to the next chart, he said, "It may look strange to have both FORGIVENESS and INVESTMENT principles next to each other, but they have a great deal in common. Both require UNDERSTANDING!"

8. FORGIVENESS
To understand others.

Lee paused for a moment, taking time to look at each person in the room, then he smiled mischievously. "I must admit that I used to worry a lot about whether I was truly forgiving. Since getting into this program, one of the best things I have learned is an entirely new outlook on forgiveness. It is said that there are only two kinds of people in the world -- *those I like and those I don't understand.* I found it hard to believe that the only reason we need to forgive is because we judge others, and the only reason we judge others is because we do not understand their point of view.

George and Shirley, we won't go into this important subject tonight because it is a course we have almost all by itself. I promise you that when we have the training on forgiveness, it will help you find more joy and satisfaction in all of your relationships, including the one you have with yourself."

9. INVESTMENT
To sow in order to reap.

"The INVESTMENT PRINCIPLE is also based upon understanding. It says, **'In the beginning you do more than what you get paid for, but in the end, you get paid for more than you do.'** Here we find another one of life's principles which sharing accentuates. In any business, it takes some time to build a foundation for a successful organization.

"As more and more players join the team, the friendships and opportunities to contribute begin to multiply. It takes hard work and dedication to build the foundation of your organization. In the beginning, your rewards and sense of fulfillment may seem small compared to your efforts. Even so, if the foundation is solid, the organization will reach a point where it will expand much more quickly than it could through your efforts alone. Once again, the financial rewards are a natural by-product. At a certain point, the organization will grow to where it generates a healthy income. A stable organization of dedicated players will continue to generate substantial overrides, month after month. And it's at this point you begin to get paid for more than what you do.

"So the investment principle says, 'Be in CONTRIBUTION for the long haul.' Life is an ongoing experience. Set long-range plans. Remember, we get out of life exactly what we give!" Lee turns the flip chart again.

10. CONTRIBUTION
To make a difference.

"The last letter is C which stands for the basic theme of our company, CONTRIBUTION. Most of us feel that we must have been put on this earth for a reason, and that reason must be to make a difference, to nurture and contribute to the quality of life in our sphere of influence.

"The CONTRIBUTION PRINCIPLE says, **'In life we get what we give.'** That is why some people get so much out of life. They merely take advantage of the unlimited opportunities to contribute to others. We could subtitle this principle, 'Sharing and Caring.' And who doesn't want to be shared with and cared for? Again, we're talking about basics. The fact is, others want you to share your life with them. They want you to care for them.

"The phrase, living is giving, comes to mind, as well as the story of the two seas in the Holy Land. The Sea of Galilee is fed by rivers and streams. It receives their contribution and passes it on. **It receives, it gives, it lives.** The Sea of Galilee is a living sea.

"On the other hand, the Dead Sea is fed by rivers and streams, but rather than passing the water on, it keeps it only to become stagnant and dead. The Dead Sea does not give and it does not live.

"We have the same alternatives with our own lives. If we give, we live. And the more we give, the more we receive. We have all heard that the one who teaches is the one who learns the most. Another way to put it is: **When we make a difference in another person's life, an even greater difference is made in our own.**

"Remember how sharing accelerates life when we come from CONTRIBUTION rather than SURVIVAL. Most people come from: 'After I get, I'll give. When I get what I want, I'll be able to give to others.'

"What doesn't work is: Receive, then give.

"What does work is: Give, then receive.

"Give, then receive -- the precious circle.

"If we don't take on a great hobby, like this, which is such a great opportunity to contribute and a great financial opportunity, as well, where will each of us be emotionally and financially five years from now? We are making up our minds to invest in ourselves, to invest in others, to take this path of responsibility, this path which tends to mold and shape us into leaders and contributors. We accept the responsibility of life and the difference it can make.

"By being all that we can be, we can lead the way for all of those who are fortunate enough to cross our paths. Life allows us to duplicate our empowerment through example, and that is the subject of our investment rule.

The Greatest Home Based Business in the World

"It has many levels of meaning, I understand, but basically it is that one must sow the seed and till the ground before the harvest. In the beginning of any project, we must work far more than we are paid, so that in the future we can be paid for more than we work. The inner principle here is patience and persistence. So let's review and read each line."

1. **STRUCTURING**
   To make change a necessity.
2. **COMMITMENT**
   To choose to get a job done.
3. **EMPOWERMENT**
   To keep my word.
4. **ENTHUSIASM**
   To be playful.
5. **NOURISHING**
   To acknowledge everyone's WINS.
6. **TRUE VALUE**
   Giving and receiving value.
7. **IMAGINATION**
   To see goals vividly.
8. **FORGIVENESS**
   To understand others.
9. **INVESTMENT**
   To sow in order to reap.
10. **CONTRIBUTION**
    To make a difference.

The Principles of Accelerated Winning

Lee Chin closed up the flip chart and said, "I want to acknowledge how each of you have made this experience one of the most enjoyable that I have ever had. It has been a great privilege to review these principles to such wonderful people as the Seekers, and the four of us are looking forward to a great relationship with you. Let's take a break now. I believe Shirley has some very special refreshments for us. Then we can get to work on the Seekers' Game Plan for the fulfillment of their dreams."

The Greatest Home Based Business in the World

The world stands aside to let anyone pass who knows where he is going.

David Starr Jordan

CHAPTER ELEVEN...

DARING TO DREAM AGAIN

After Shirley Seeker had served her delicious hot apple pie, Lee Chin let out a happy chuckle and said, "George and Shirley, this is the most exciting part for all of us. We are going to help you design your GAME PLAN for getting to where you really want to go. Since Harold and Claudia are going to be your Team Managers, they will be working the most directly with you, so Harold has agreed to lead this part of our session."

Harold began, leaning forward in his chair, "As we mentioned earlier, when we were telling you about ourselves, we shared how each of us is daring to dream big again. We told you brief descriptions of some of those dreams with you. So, now, Shirley, would you tell us about your own background, what you enjoy doing most of all and what you would like to accomplish?"

As she began talking, everyone listened intently. Shirley acknowledged that her special talent had been in music, and she had given up a promising career when the children came. Even with the help of some pointed questioning from Harold, it took her time to identify that her greatest inspiration had happened at a summer camp for young musicians. As a result, she used to dream about being able to establish such a camp for gifted, underprivileged teenagers.

The group helped her revitalize that dream so that she could visualize the people, buildings, scenery and activities. Her heart began to pound as she realized how such a dream might now be accomplished. Such a goal would take plenty of time and money, which in the past had made it nothing but a fantasy. But now there was a way to get both the time and the money.

George's turn came next. He reviewed the things he had told The Winner and how he had always wanted to teach leadership and management, then added, "While listening to Shirley and her summer camp, I got an idea that gives me goose bumps. During the summer we could use the camp for the kids, but the rest of the year we could have leadership training seminars. The Principles of Accelerated Winning are so powerfully simple. I know how the concept of going from SUR-

VIVAL to CONTRIBUTION has already made a difference in the way I am looking at things. This whole concept of individual empowerment through commitment and integrity is something most of us need to be far more conscious of. Do you realize how lives could be transformed?"

Harold exclaimed, "I'm getting your goose bumps, too. How does that sound to you Shirley?"

Shirley loved the idea. Within the next fifteen minutes, while everyone in the room added their exciting suggestions, the Seekers began to visualize just where, when and how they could establish the mountain retreat. With the help of Harold's thought provoking questions, a specific plan was adopted. A five year target date was set, with a personal, half-million dollar net worth and a $20,000 per month independent income to keep it funded. Shirley's renewal of that old, almost forgotten, dream was becoming so real that a few tears of joy swelled up in her eyes.

"Shirley and George," Harold said, looking at them both very intently, "my wife and I want to add our very serious commitment toward your goal. We intend to see that you have the income to make that dream come true. We will work hard to assist you in becoming an effective creator and manager of a large, successful organization."

At this point, Harold asked Lee Chin to share with the Seekers what he had previously taught them about COMMITMENT COACHING.

Lee said he would be delighted and briefly took over. "George, my wife has told me many times how much she enjoys working under your leadership at the office. It is no wonder you would like to run a management and leadership school. And Shirley, I can tell by your lovely home that you are a good manager too."

Shirley acknowledged the compliment but laughingly insisted that consistency was not one of her major assets.

As the group smiled at her candid honesty, Lee continued. "What is so powerful about our Ten Scientific Principles of Accelerated Winning is that as we start living by them, we start managing our organization by them too. We call it COMMITMENT COACHING. This approach to leadership will prove very valuable in building and managing your organization."

George interrupted, "Lee, could you explain how Commitment Coaching is different from what we usually mean by Management by Objective?"

Lee grinned, "You bet. Commitment Coaching is a powerful way to implement Management by Objective. It does so by three very simple rules which are so obvious that we often overlook them in supporting and supervising others. Here they are:

1. Specific, step-by-step, mutually understood goals. Help your people set up and commit to clearly defined day by day goals, not just the long term objectives.

2. Find and communicate what is working. Give

frequent compliments by acknowledging each little WIN.

3. Give clear reprimands when needed, with reassurance. When commitments are not fulfilled, hold people accountable with firmness, but also with reassurance that you appreciate them and find it a privilege to be working with them."

Harold thanked Lee for defining Commitment Coaching and then continued, "As you can tell, George and Shirley, my wife and I are excited about your five year goal. As we all know, your dreams will require full dedication and hard work. We want to assist you to do in five years what most people would never accomplish in forty. Obviously, there will be those times of discouragement when you will want to slack off or even quit. Our commitment to you is that we will be there with you all the way. It is our determination to keep you focused and on target until your dream is a reality. My wife and I are willing to take on the personal responsibility of being your Commitment Coaches. But to do so, we are asking you if you want us to be your hardball coach in the Accelerated Game of Life.

"We can only do so if you desire us to hold you to account for your commitments. That means there will be those times when we will hold your feet to the fire. It won't always be fun or convenient. In fact, there may be times when you might wish we would dry up and blow away. But our promise to you is that we will not give up on you, if that is what you really want."

Harold's voice took on a very serious but friendly tone. Claudia was grinning, nodding her head in full agreement, as her husband challenged their newest Team members. Harold then said in conclusion, "So, Shirley and George, we want you to think very carefully. Do both of you want us to be your Commitment Coaches?"

The Seekers were moved by the seriousness of the challenge. They both liked the Johnsons. They knew they were absolutely serious. Yes, certainly the road would be rough at times, but there was no question that teamwork would greatly enhance the possibility of success.

Shirley spoke first, with a little moisture building up in her eyes. "We haven't known you before tonight, but I personally acknowledge that with the all-out commitment you have made to us, I want both of you to be my coach and be as tough as you have to be to keep me working toward our goal."

George surprised himself by being a little choked up too, but covering it with his grin, he responded, "This whole shift in our life is the most exciting thing that has happened to us in a long time. I want to thank you both for taking us on. I promise you that if I start goofing off, you have my permission to do what you need to do to get me back on track."

"Fantastic!" Harold exclaimed. "We are making a total commitment to you and your terrific goals. We are very serious about that. Now let me tell you what we need to do first." Harold picked up Lee's flip chart and turned over a page, reading out loud the following six steps:

STEPS TO GETTING STARTED:

1. Complete Application to become an Independent Marketing Associate.

2. Establish sponsoring and training schedule and goals.

3. Start a Special People List.

4. Start clearly defining and listing the things which you want to BE, DO, HAVE, and CONTRIBUTE for each period.

5. Go over the steps with your Team Manager and sign the associated commitments.

6. Start making appointments for your 'Two on One' recruiting sessions.

Harold continued, "Our first step is to set a timetable for sponsoring your three key players. Claudia and I set our goal to have our first three in ten days.

"We had our first two in six days and Irene and Lee are assigning you to us, so our 'Executive Team' is complete. We want to help you achieve the same ten day goal. Then, in turn, we want to help your three get their people in ten days.

"You can see how rapidly we can build your Primary Team if we recognize the urgency of going full-out. So are you ready to make a solid commitment to do whatever is necessary to have your first three in place in ten days?"

George looked at Shirley, nodding his head up and down. "We can do it! It probably couldn't come at a busier time, but this has got to take priority."

"Wonderful. This business is so easy when you do it fast. It's hard only if you do it slowly. We will have two to three months of intensive work getting your organization established in depth and trained. Lee has been working the pants off us the last ten days and we are going to do the same for you. That's the way we make it work.

"As for training, we have company tapes and literature, starting with your Kit."

Harold laid out the literature and went over the various materials. A list of tapes were reviewed, checking the ones the Seekers wanted right away. Harold would deliver them on Monday, at which time a schedule for listening to the tapes would be agreed upon. Next, Harold looked at his Calendar which showed what training seminars were scheduled. The Seekers checked their own Day Planners to see which of the training events they could attend. They also were shown when the next big Monthly Forum Meeting was going to be and agreed to clear their calendar for that event.

"All of a sudden," George mused, "this is beginning to look like a lot of time."

Harold smiled broadly, "We all have the time to do what we REALLY want, and you folks REALLY want to have that fantastic music and leadership retreat, don't you?"

"Yes, thank you, Harold," George replied. "I know that we must keep in mind the commitment to make that dream a reality. Okay, what else have you got for us?"

Harold reached over and grabbed the back of George's neck and chuckled as he gave it a squeeze. "We are also busy with our business and family obligations George, and we want all of us to make this network business a lot of fun. Have you noticed how much fun this has been tonight?"

"Fantastic!" Shirley exclaimed.

"Our third step is to have you start making your Special People List of those you would most like on your first-level."

A list was started and soon had nine names on it. As George and Shirley identified each person with a little description, everyone's excitement continued to grow.

Lee Chin finally exclaimed, "I knew the Seekers would have some good contacts, but these people are really outstanding. You guys are going to do fabulously well!"

Harold then said, "Okay, you have the idea of the Special People List. I want you to build that list up to at least twenty-five and then prioritize the names. Pick the three that you want on your Executive Team. I can be over on Monday at 5:00 o'clock to bring the tapes. Can you have the list for me by then?"

"Sure," George agreed, "I'll do my darndest!"

"NO!" Harold responded. "I don't want to know if you will do your darndest. I want to know if you will Commit to having it for me at 5:00 o'clock. Will you?"

Harold's face was serious and he was looking George directly in the eye, fulfilling the role of a Commitment Coach. He was being firm but fair.

George, nodding his head, replied, "I see what you mean," grinning. "Okay, I will definitely have it for you Monday at 5:00 PM."

"Great," Harold said, with a big, smiling chuckle and turning to Lee. "You see, I'm beginning to catch on to this, after all."

Lee laughed and confided to George, "I had to knock down about half a dozen of his 'I'll try' commitments."

Harold surprised the Seekers with his next instruction. "Now, George and Shirley, I want you to promise me that you will not try to sponsor anyone on this list."

Shirley looked the most shocked and said, "Why in the world not? I thought that is why we are making up the list. You've got to be kidding!"

Harold assured her that he was serious. He explained, "Generally speaking, friends resist being challenged and awakened by people they know well. It is very easy for them to become defensive and you can lose them. It is much better to let a 'stranger' be the teacher. Does that make sense to you?"

Shirley answered, thoughtfully nodding her head, "Wow! You are so right. That makes a lot of sense."

Then Harold added, "Monday, when I come over, I will show you how easy it is to make appointments for the two of us to visit with these people. I will assist you and then you will assist your people. We call it **Two-on-One Recruiting Magic.** Hold Monday evening open. We may be able to get things started then."

"Our next step is to get you on a track of using **Positive Expressions with Imagination.** You remember that one of the key Principles of Accelerated Winning was IMAGINATION. Have either of you tried to use what is often called Positive Affirmations before?"

"I did," George answered, "after reading *Think and Grow Rich* by Napoleon Hill. I am sure that it helped, but I didn't stay with it."

"I understand," Harold said. "A lot of us have had the same problem. The most successful people I know have used affirmations to move them from mediocrity to greatness, but they all stress that doing it consistently, with feeling, is the key.

"We take the idea of affirmations a few steps further. First of all, we call them 'Expressions' because we are doing more than affirming something. We are sending out a conscious, deliberate statement to the universe and our incredible subconscious. We express these as OUR INTENTION in positive, present tense declarations. We start out using seven very powerful expressions. We are repeating them every day with feeling and visualization. It doesn't take long to notice a difference."

Irene Chin interrupted, "I believe these positive expressions have done more for me than anything else. I started out by taking four or five minutes to visualize myself being what is expected in each statement. Now I do them in half a minute."

Harold continued, "Here is a copy of your new POSITIVE EXPRESSIONS. Let's read them over and see if they describe your desired self-image."

POSITIVE EXPRESSIONS:

1. I experience WINNING at everything I set out to do.
2. I enjoy being enthusiastic and have an abundance of energy at all times.
3. I plan and organize my time daily and carefully follow my plan through to completion.
4. I rejoice in the success of others.
5. I am grateful, serene, relaxed, compassionate, expressive, empowering and purposeful.
6. I love to serve and nurture others, to empower them to expand, to help others enhance the quality of their lives.
7. I trust in a Higher Power! I believe in myself and I dare to dream.

Harold now explained, "These expressions were carefully selected to provide valuable subconscious support in very specific areas. How do you like them,

Shirley?"

"Using such expressions is new to me," she answered, "but I can see the need to reprogram my old conditioning with a more positive self-image. I am anxious to try them."

George stated, "I like the way they deal with 'being' and 'doing' rather than getting. I am delighted to see you are including Positive Expressions in our program."

Lee Chin thanked him for his appreciation and then made an announcement. "As a finishing note, we have some great news. I'll let Irene tell you about it."

Irene was beaming. "I have a wonderful announcement for all of you. The Winner is home for this weekend and is inviting all of those who have joined in the last two weeks to come to his house for a special orientation.

"The time is tomorrow night at 7:30 PM. All four of you are invited and, believe me, whatever it takes to be there, don't miss it. Lee and I attended a month ago and wouldn't have missed it for the world.

"I need to let his wife, Jean, know who will be there."

Shirley let out a happy shriek, exclaiming, "Ever since George told me of his visit with The Winner, I have been anxious to meet him. We'll be there, won't we George?" George nodded with a great deal of agreement and satisfaction. The Johnson's were happy about being there too.

The Greatest Home Based Business in the World

Lee Chin again thanked everyone for making it such a memorable evening, especially, their great hosts, the Seekers.

George Seeker returned the thanks and then turned to all four guests.

"I would like to say something, especially to the Chins. A week ago our life was in the doldrums. Yes, we once had big dreams, but our lives had actually betrayed those dreams. Thanks to you folks, we are on fire again. We are not only a lot clearer as to what we REALLY want, but, even more thrilling, we now see a way to make it possible. We really do appreciate this evening and the time you have all spent. Irene, you are a real doll. Lee, you did absolutely great. Both Shirley and I are so very impressed with our new sponsors. We are really going to enjoy being players on your team."

There were some sincere hugs and thanks. True to Irene's promise, it had been a very remarkable evening.

CHAPTER TWELVE...

A PLAYER'S NATURAL PROGRESSION
"Walk before you run"

There was no question about the excitement as the people filled the spacious family room at The WINNER's house. Everyone felt honored by being invited. Both The Winner and his wife cordially welcomed them as they arrived, giving each a personally engraved name tag. Shirley was a little surprised that The Winner was shorter and leaner than her husband.

At exactly 7:30, Jean walked to the front of the crowded room and extended her welcome. "My husband and I are so pleased that you could make it tonight on such short notice. It has been about a year now that this wonderful change has been taking place in our home. I want to admit that I was very skeptical about all this talk that a friend began sharing with us about **WINNING through CONTRIBUTION.** But when I saw the change that was taking place in my husband's life, I decided to pay more attention. I think my problem, ever since my youth, was that I fed off of being a 'drama queen,' always talking about how bad things were for me. I felt I was a victim of so many circumstances. And I want you to know that it was not easy for me to see how I hid behind blaming others, giving up my power to change."

Every eye in the room was riveted upon the gracious, smiling speaker. As she paused, taking a big breath and beaming from ear to ear, she declared softly, "Now, life is such a privilege. Life is such a miracle. I could never see it before because I felt my world was so unfair and imperfect. What I have finally discovered is that nothing out there makes any difference. Really! It all depends upon our point of view, our inner expression."

The room exploded with spontaneous applause. Many of those present did not really understand the depth of her words, but they did "get" that, somehow, she had found a new meaning to life.

Jean, having finished, began to move from in front of the room when The Winner caught her with his extended hand and, with his arm around her waist, led her back to the front of the group.

A Player's Natural Progression

"Folks, the greatest thrill I have had this last year is watching this lovely jewel discover her incredible magnificence. Thank you darling, for waiting for me to finally grow up so that I, too, could be more like a child."

Responding to an even louder round of applause, Jean, radiant and beaming, left The WINNER's side and went to the back of the room. The Winner looked at his guests and asked, "How many of you feel that since joining our Company, your life is starting to blossom?"

Everyone showed agreement by their laughing acknowledgment and applause.

"Well, folks," The Winner commenced, "the best way to stay awake is to help others stay awake. It is much harder to go back to sleep when you are helping others awaken to greater aliveness. This is vital because the Accelerated Game of Life will also accentuate fear, frustration, failure, etc. It doesn't miss a lick. It's all there -- life, in general. I firmly believe that a person playing the Accelerate Game full-out can experience in several years what most people do in a normal lifetime."

LIFE RUNS IN CYCLES

"Actually, life, especially the Accelerated Game of Life, is a continual progression, but it does go in cycles -- highs and lows -- ups and downs. It is said that the only thing in life which is constant is change! This being true, 'All things must pass.' In other words, if you are currently experiencing your lowest or highest point in life, it is only a passing phenomena. The redeeming factor about these life cycles is that they tend to keep moving upward. **Not only can the highs get higher, but the lows can get higher as well.**

"When we start flowing with life, our lives naturally progress toward enlightenment, fulfillment and satisfaction. What happens naturally is for our lives to work. And sometimes, when they don't appear to be working, it's only because we're trying to force things to happen, trying to play hardball with softball rules.

"Why do we try to play hardball with softball rules? I think the answer is so simple that we miss it. The answer is that from the day we were born, we bought into the idea that the purpose of living is to be comfortable, to gain pleasure and escape pain. Isn't that true?"

He waited for the majority of heads to nod in agreement.

"But if that is true, then what would have happened if we had never experienced any discomfort or pain of any kind? If I were all powerful, and as you might suppose, all loving, so that I could have so blessed you that you would have never, ever, known physical, emotional, psychological or spiritual pain throughout your entire life, I want each of you to think very carefully as to what you would be like today? Can anyone here tell me?"

The audience was quiet for a moment and then a few hands went up.

"We would be incapable of comprehending life,"

A Player's Natural Progression

one offered.

"We could not understand others or be compassionate toward them," another volunteered.

Several more added similar observations. Most in the room were shaking their heads in agreement, while a few had puzzled looks on their faces.

The Winner continued, "So we see, waking up means discovering that life was not designed to be about comfort alone, although we want a goodly portion of it, of course. Life is not about getting to some destination. It's about the journey. It's not about getting something - it's about becoming something.

"Life is about growth through all kinds of experiences. Every experience in life, if seen for its real value, is a win. In the light of this, if you go back and carefully examine your life, SUCCESS IS ALL YOU HAVE EVER KNOWN.

"When you grasp this great myth about your past, you begin to see more and more real value in all the things happening in the present - in everything that is happening this moment. As in the past, they may or may not be comfortable, but they all have value.

"When you more fully experience how this principle of value is true for the present, then you begin to realize that it certainly is going to be true in the future, and BINGO! You just hit the jackpot.

"As Jean just told us, 'Life is now such a privilege and a continuous miracle.'

"If we can really see that life flows in a natural,

upward progression, what works for us, as players, is to go with the flow. Another colloquial way to put it is: 'We have to walk before we can run'."

DUPLICATION PRINCIPLE

"So, as I said, the way to stay awake is to assist others in staying awake. We call it the DUPLICATION PRINCIPLE because by sharing your own aliveness with others, you perpetuate it in yourself. It won't work any other way. **What you keep, diminishes. What you give away, multiplies.**

"No matter how effective and successful you try to be in life, you'll contribute the most by being duplicatable. There is a simple rule to duplicating yourself. It is called KEEPING IT SIMPL. The more complicated you and your techniques are, the harder it will be to duplicate yourself.

"You may sponsor Sara and contribute greatly to her, but if she can't duplicate the same for Jerry, the process stops.

"For an enthusiastic organization to continue to grow, the sponsoring, training and motivation must be simple and duplicatable. Since there is no limit to how many times you can duplicate yourself, 'the sky is the limit'. Your organization can continue to grow and your commission checks can continue to increase. They depend only on how well you and your associates duplicate yourselves.

"And what is the most duplicatable? What is the

A Player's Natural Progression

simplest? The answer is obvious. All of us can duplicate honesty, sincerity and integrity. If we 'talk straight,' tell it like it is, and avoid the tendency to exaggerate and 'sell the sizzle,' then we will be easily and naturally duplicated."

STAGES OF PROGRESSION

"So wouldn't it be great to know what stages you will go through as you progress? Sure it would, and it's only fair that you do. Therefore, let's take a look.

"I know most of you are already excited about building your teams, but I invited you here tonight to give you perspective. I have found it very helpful to identify the stages through which each of you will progress in building your organizations. Your awareness of these stages will subdue your tendency 'to get the cart before the horse.' You will be able to proceed one step at a time, lay a solid foundation and not be easily discouraged. Many times we become discouraged when we're only on page thirty while wanting to be on page fifty, and not knowing that page thirty is exactly where we should be.

"I have a little chart which shows the natural stages of progression in building our teams and how these stages relate to our various ages. Of course, these associated ages and time periods are only approximations."

The Winner put the following chart on an easel:

STAGE	LIFETIME
Formative	0 - 6 years
Concentration	6 - 20 years
Momentum	20 - 50 years
Stability	50+ years

"Since I like to use allegories from sports, we might say that to score you have to touch all four bases. In other words, we can't get to STABILITY without completing the three prior stages. Let's take them one at a time and see how they relate more specifically to building your own organization."

FORMATIVE STAGE

"What we experienced for about the first six years of our life was our Formative Stage, where the mind patterns we created dramatically affect our entire life. Your first four weeks in this business could be called your Formative Stage. It is that period of time when you are learning about how to use the products, understanding the Compensation Program, establishing your Game Plan and sponsoring your three key players.

"This Formative Stage is the blueprint from which your organization is built and the structure within which to operate.

"Get the picture? The Formative Stage is the

A Player's Natural Progression

ATHLETE	NETWORKING
Little League	1 - 4 weeks
School League	1 - 2 years
Minor League	3 - 5 years
Major League	Financial Independence

shortest period, yet it's the most critical since it lays the track on which to run. That is what you have been doing so far. Our purpose tonight is to continue that process by coaching you in formulating the attitudes, habits, actions, purposes and plans which will work best for you."

CONCENTRATION STAGE

"While we were receiving our education and growing into adulthood from about ages six through twenty, we all went through the Concentration Stage. In this business, it is where we get the ball rolling. It's the time to 'make hay while the sun shines'. And, as my mother used to say, 'Anything, worth doing, is worth doing right.' And doing it right usually takes time.

"The length of time for this stage can be accomplished in about six months of concentrated effort before you can go at a more leisurely pace. The important thing to realize is that your foundation is built during this stage. The future quality and integrity of your teams are set up during this period.

"Some of you may want to exert an intense effort for a shorter time, but, for most, this takes the fun out of it. It becomes more like work than a hobby, and the tendency is to 'burn oneself out'.

"Remember, the more realistic and long-term approach is that of a hobby. You don't have to create an organization overnight. Yet, don't use that thought as an 'excuse' for not playing full-out. The point is to establish a comfortable, long-distance pace. The successful approach to life is that of a marathon runner rather than that of a sprinter.

"The first part of the Concentration Stage is where you start building and working depth in your Primary Team. When your organization starts growing exponentially, you'll have the organizational foundation from which the Momentum Stage can begin.

"The time involved for the Concentration Stage varies with the quality of leadership and the commitment of the players. An organization, built around strong leadership, which is duplicated and which contains a high percentage of serious players, will find itself in MOMENTUM long before an organization lacking these attributes."

MOMENTUM STAGE

"Just as our first six years in life became the basis of our growing up during the school years, the first thirty years of our adult life is spent becoming established.

A Player's Natural Progression

"By following your plan, you build your foundation during the Concentration Stage. Then, the Momentum Stage takes over. It is where the 'shell of the building' begins to quickly take shape. All of a sudden you begin to see compounding results. All of a sudden the structure of your growing nationwide organization becomes visible.

"Prior to MOMENTUM, you experience 'doing more than what you get paid for'. There seems to be very little visible results. But once the Momentum Stage gets underway, you begin to experience that part of the investment principle which is 'getting paid for more than what you do'. Finally, we begin to see really significant results.

"In other words, once a properly built team reaches a certain size, it seems to explode. The organization flows from Concentration to Momentum automatically. If you are consistently building a solid, duplicatable foundation which is based upon straight-talk and integrity, at some point you will recognize Momentum. Perhaps you will suddenly realize that your team is growing by leaps and bounds, and that the growth seems to be effortless. That's Momentum. It's exciting, but, like everything else, it is not necessarily permanent.

"The longer you operate within the Concentration Stage, the longer the Momentum Stage will last. Consequently, the Momentum Stage can be extended in proportion to your period of concentrated effort. Furthermore, Momentum can be renewed by another period of concentrated effort.

"By spending six months in the Concentration phase, your Momentum should last another six to eighteen months. Even during the Momentum Stage, you need to 'ongoingly' provide coaching and set an example for your team.

"Momentum is exhilarating. Flow with it and enjoy every moment."

STABILITY STAGE

"That period in life after fifty years of age is what most people experience as the Stability Stage. In our example of progressive stages in this business, the Stability Stage is where your purpose is fulfilled for designing and constructing the building.

"Regarding your teams, the Stability Stage will still involve gradual improvements, not just maintenance. Here you experience a gradual growth and expansion of your whole organization. Remember, life's natural tendency is improvement and expansion. In other words, mere maintenance in life is unstable.

"For those who have built their organizations around contribution, the Stability Stage can provide a financial freedom and life-style second to none. The beauty of it all, and the reason it provides freedom, is because your income can be independent of risk capital, overhead, employees, inventories, complicated accounting, working for someone else, a rigid work schedule (8 to 5), etc.

"To a certain degree, the Stability Stage provides an income which is independent of you. We call it 'residual' income. You may travel around the world with your family and return to find that your organization and income are larger. But that's not to say that during the Stability Stage you can become less responsible. Your organization may require less time and be less demanding but the need for your leadership and coaching will continue.

Remember, life's natural tendency is expansion. Mere maintenance in life, or networking, is unstable. In other words, a flat line (maintenance) or a downward trending line (contraction) is unstable in life and networking.

STABILITY

MAINTENANCE

CONTRACTION

"The Stability Stage is truly the 'big carrot' in team building. We have all heard about those in network marketing around the country who are successful and enjoy an incredible life-style. Their lives revolve around travel, communicating and making a difference. Most of their travel expenses are tax deductible, and they get paid for doing something that is both enjoyable and rewarding.

"The payoff includes much more than just money. Their opportunities for personal growth are unlimited. Their opportunities to contribute to others are unlimited. They operate within a structure that is the precious circle of giving and receiving. Their lives are powerful and empowering.

"By the way, I've been talking about you! Your heart cries out to contribute in a big way. I see you there. See yourself there, commit to being there, and follow the Game Plan I will explain next. The Game Plan is like a roadway to, into and through each stage of the process."

CHAPTER THIRTEEN...

ESTABLISHING A GAME PLAN

"So far, I have given you a 'bird's eye view' of the building process and the approximate length of time associated with each stage. Now, we are going to proceed through each stage step-by-step."

Setting the Goals and laying the Track in the Formative Stage.

"As you recall, the formulative stage is the time you design the ultimate integrity, the bottom line of your team. In your networking career, this is the stage where your blueprint is created. Everything in the physical universe began as an idea or thought. Each of your teams will be just as strong, or just as weak, as you design them to be.

"By taking the small amount of time required to design your future, and, by putting it down in black and white, you will automatically be a quantum leap ahead of the crowd. Who would consider trying to build a large, multifaceted, high-rise office complex without a blueprint? The answer, of course, is no one! By the same token, who would consider building a large, multifaceted, complex organization without a blueprint? Oddly enough, the answer is almost everyone!

"Can you believe it? Why would anyone even try to build something without the foggiest idea of what it is supposed to look like? The fact is that most people approach life this way.

"Absolutely essential for you to get from where you are now to where you want to be, is to know where you want to be. Once you've decided where, you must know how to get there. Since the 'how' probably involves knowledge, method, time, effort and expense, you must be willing to do whatever it takes to get there. I'm talking about a commitment - a no alternative, 'burn your bridges behind you' commitment. The rest is history. You will get there. The universe works that way.

"Personally, I believe that the universe was set up to honor any and all clearly defined intentions which are backed by absolute commitment."

TAKING A STAND

"Now is the time to take a stand to be different. You can't afford to follow the crowd! The price is your life! Throughout history the masses have collected evidence that life doesn't work, that they are at the 'effect' of circumstances rather than 'cause'. Now is the time to take a stand on the evidence collected by those whose lives work. The following is what they discover about themselves:

Establishing a Game Plan

- I am a whole, capable, adequate and complete individual.
- The smarter I work, not the harder I work, the more money I make.
- I live in a universe of abundance rather than scarcity.
- My commitment is to have the sufficiency to contribute abundantly.

"Those people whose lives work this way are no different from anyone else. The difference, in results, has to do with intention and commitment. To produce outstanding results with your life, you may only need to design a specific, written plan and make a no-alternative, 'burn your bridges behind you' commitment. It works in Life. And besides, if you're not playing fully committed, you have no chance to win -- zero!

"What you are learning in building and supporting your team can be applied to all aspects of life.

"So, this first month, while you are in the Formative Stage, you have been deciding where you want to be. As you complete your Game Plan, you are creating a track which will carry you to your 6 month, 12 month, 3 year, 6 year and 10 year destinations. Those of you who have not done so yet, make this a first priority. Without a track to run on and a destination to move toward, your life will be spent on detours to nowhere.

"The destinations are your desires, and the track is your commitment to contribute. In other words, the most direct path to what you want is to contribute to others.

"Here's what I consider to be a universal law:

The way to tap into the flow of universal abundance is to come from contribution and be absolutely committed to specific, written intentions.

In other words, write down a plan involving contribution and take a stand on it."

MAKING AND KEEPING COMMITMENTS

"Making commitments and keeping them are essential for life to work. Without commitment, life is death. To experience 'aliveness' we must commit ourselves to projects and purposes which make a contribution. But not only do we have to make commitments, we have to keep them. If you don't keep your commitments, your life will not work. If you do, it will. It's just that simple.

"Talk about hope -- talk about excitement -- talk about taking the pressure off! If you can accept the evidence that I've collected about how simple life is, you're going to be ecstatic. Evidence has proven to me that a life set in motion upon the right track, and kept simple, guarantees the desired results.

WE LEARN HOW TO TRANSCEND OUR 'STUFF'

"Hundreds of books have been written about positive thinking, inspiration, repetition of positive affir-

Establishing a Game Plan

mations, etc. Thousands of 'how to' books have told us that if we will do this ritual, or that ritual, we will succeed. But evidence indicates that most tips and techniques prove ineffective. They sell because a good idea is always more seductive than the truth. I know that you're about to drown in good ideas, and need to be rescued by the simple truth. And, by the way, I'm not trying to sell you anything. Truth is truth, whether you, or I, or anyone else believes it. The only things which we have to 'believe' are our judgments, opinions and prejudices which our survival mechanisms won't let go of.

"Probably, that little voice in the back of your head (your self talk) just said, 'Could that be the truth, or is that just his opinion?'

"And it doesn't matter. It doesn't matter, because who we really are is not our Survival system of opinions, beliefs, judgments, prejudices and the like (which for simplification, we'll label our stuff). Thank goodness we can transcend our 'stuff,' because we're never going to change it, no matter how many 'how to' books we read.

"Ninety percent of our 'stuff' was firmly in place by age three. Our Survival Mechanism latched onto every ounce of 'stuff' it could. The basic theme of our 'stuff' is: 'To survive I need to make others wrong and me right.' Of course, as long as we operate from our 'stuff,' we'll be trapped in the Survival circle, where life never works.

"Oops! There it goes again -- that little voice

saying, 'Why doesn't he get to the point.' Well, here it is. The simple truth is:

" Life works! Being in the flow of abundance is natural. The river of abundance flows in the realm of Contribution, but not in the realm of Survival. To go with the flow, we merely need to flip our mental switch from Survival to Contribution, observe our 'stuff' but not let it run us, and build a boat to ride in."

"The boat is merely the track which we are going to create as we proceed. It might clarify this concept to think of this track as a STRUCTURE within which to operate, a structure that keeps you within the realm of contribution. We'll design this Structure in such a way that it will keep you flowing with contribution, like the walls of a 'water slide' channel the water and you right to a big splash.

"What we want to do is create a Structure or track which will automatically transport you to making a big splash in life. All you need do is 'push off'. Gravity will take care of the rest.

"I hope that where we're headed is clear, and, in case it's not I'll summarize:

> 1. Your life will work automatically, as long as you come from a commitment to contribute.
>
> 2. You can't get rid of your 'stuff'. It will try to keep you in Survival. Your 'self talk' will keep telling you that your life doesn't work. But your willingness to CONTRIBUTE allows you to operate outside of your 'stuff'. It allows you to

Establishing a Game Plan

be big enough to observe your 'stuff' and tell that little voice in your head, 'Thanks for sharing, but my life does work.'

3. Your precise, black and white, written statement of who you are, who you're going to be, and how you're going to get there, creates a track with guardrails which prevent derailment. Of course, your 'stuff' tries to get you off track, but, as you trend that way, the guardrails slap you right in the face -- a rude awakening, but exactly what you needed and wanted.

"So, let's start laying your track. It will be laid in stages. As we get into the Concentration phase, we will lay down some commitments regarding sponsoring, supporting your organization, etc.

"Even though we may look at it in different ways, and in more depth as we proceed, it seems appropriate to discuss another truth at this time. And this is the "biggy"! This is the one which will transform your life. The more you align yourself with this one, the more difference you are going to make. And here it is:

"The only way to stay in the realm of contribution is to sponsor others into it!

"Personally sponsoring and helping your people to sponsor is the front line - it keeps you in the game. By the way, it's the only game in town. For, in all of life, you will be conned into believing people's excuses, or you will sponsor them into the realm of Contribution.

Every day you either let people sell you on why they should stay in their 'stuff,' or you sponsor them. You 'sell out,' or you make a difference. We cannot experience transformation in our own lives without participating in the transformation of others.

"So, your stand should be to sponsor others into the realm of Contribution. And a stand is like the Alamo -- this is it, to the end! The more people you recruit, the more contribution becomes a part of you, and, not only does your capacity to contribute expand, but it becomes increasingly easier to stay on track.

"By now, the big picture should be taking shape. You should be starting to comprehend the magnitude of what we're doing. We're not just sponsoring others into our business. We're sponsoring them into life itself. Sponsoring is merely a 'modus operandi' which allows us to make the transition from the land of the living-dead (Survival) to the land of aliveness (Contribution).

"Could we possibly have a more noble purpose in life? Of course not! And the 'icing on the cake' is the fact that sponsoring allows us to not only earn a better living, but to even tap into the universal flow of abundance. Wow! I'm excited! It's such a thrill to have been able to transcend 'stuff' long enough to have recognized sponsoring for what it really is, to tell you about it and to contribute it to you.

"At this point, there is very little doubt in my mind about your desire and willingness to take the first step. It's now time to 'push off'. It's time to 'swing out'. It's time to take your stand."

COMMITMENT

"The quality of what we do after completing the FORMATIVE STAGE will be determined by the quality you've already designed into it. And, you might note that there aren't different qualities of commitments. You either commit, or you don't. So what do you do if you didn't go full-out? Bring your integrity all the way up for this, and if it's necessary, go back and rework your formative stage.

"Think big; create big; play big. Swing out there and be big. Step way out there and burn those bridges. After all, you're going to find your life, and you're going to win.

"The key to your commitment is your willingness to commit your people on the same basis you commit yourself. Here are the rules:

1. Each person is personally responsible for his own commitment and for providing his Team Manager with 'proof positive' of such.

2. Each person is personally responsible to keep at least three committed people first-level.

3. Each person monitors his organization through three generations. He is ultimately responsible for three first-level, nine second-level and twenty-seven third-level players. And that's it!

"You don't need to feel responsible for a team of hundreds. Just thinking about it is overwhelming. If each of us maintain integrity through three levels, the rest will take care of itself. If each of us is committed to making a difference through three generations, the entire group will benefit.

"The integrity of your teammate's commitments are based upon your letting them know the score. Here are six critical areas:

1. Everyone knows what they are up against -- they know the rules of the game, and more importantly, they know what is expected of them.

2. Everyone is aware of the costs, as well as the potential rewards.

3. Everyone at least understands the Contribution Principle and what it means to make a difference.

4. Everyone knows about the different stages through which he/she will progress.

5. Everyone has a blueprint for success, has committed to success, and supports each other in achieving success.

6. Most important of all, everyone has a game plan, a step-by-step procedure which, when followed, produces the desired results.

"To play or not to play, that is the question? And whoever answers, 'to play,' plays by the rules, full-out. Whether a player's word is as good as gold, or as worthless as a tinker's damn, becomes quite apparent at your Forum Meetings. He is either ready to go or he is not. If he needs more time, he should be transferred to your Reserve Team where you can work more intensely with him later.

"By continuing to build teams which go three-wide by three-deep while maintaining 'our' kind of commitment and integrity, you could find your organization moving into the Momentum Stage in as little as 3 to 6 months -- the time period being inversely proportional to your effort.

"One great aspect of being an entrepreneur is that we get paid what we're worth, or, as previously noted, we get out of it exactly what we put into it."

MOMENTUM STAGE

"As our concentrated effort causes our organization to move into Momentum, we begin to experience rapid growth, because no longer are we alone. We have duplicated ourselves, and the effects of geometric progression are becoming apparent.

"The Momentum Stage can be an exciting time because it seems like you have the 'tiger by the tail'. However, many people fail in leadership at this point because they become so infatuated with this phase that they lose sight of what produced it. Many things can happen psychologically, and most are bad.

"At this point, some people become convinced that they are invincible, that their organization will expand forever, and they 'bet on the come'. We might refer to this trap as the 'high-roller' syndrome. We could discuss it for hours, but the bottom line is: they spend money which they don't have. And if it doesn't come, or if it doesn't come soon enough, it's the fault of our program. They destroy their own image of our company, and, the sad part is, their organization is destroyed at the same time.

"I call the second trap the 'lost lover' syndrome. This is the situation where the person falls deeply in love with the Momentum Stage. And, believe me, it has a way of romancing you. It's an exciting relationship, but, when the 'new wears off,' he/she begins to feel neglected. Your attitude can deteriorate to the point where you feel like you have been 'dumped,' and you will want to end the relationship, meaning your involvement. What we must realize is that the new wears off of everything in life. We must be aware of it and be prepared for it.

"Yet another syndrome is one I call 'spoiled rotten'. Organizational growth is so natural and easy during the Momentum period. It's so easy, it can spoil you. You begin to think that Momentum is the way it was meant to be. You want it that way, or not at all. The tendency is to completely lose sight of what you did to create Momentum. Without an understanding of how Concentration and Momentum are interrelated, it's hard to figure out that to have more Momentum, you just go back to the basics.

"We could ramble on, but by now it's clear -- long term success demands that we never lose sight of our very simple steps. As soon as we do, it's all downhill. The main point of my message this evening is to continue:

- Coming from Contribution with Commitment.
- Setting your goals and staying on your track.
- Being loyal to our company.
- Using the products.
- Continue sponsoring, coaching and empowering.

"And that's it! Those are the basics that work every time. The only 'missing link' is whether or not you will go through the motions, which is completely within your control and your responsibility.

"So, to keep Momentum rolling, keep in touch with the basics. Keep them alive and a part of you."

YOU GET WHAT YOU GIVE!

"I want to acknowledge each of you for being a part of this great opportunity. As you know, we are out to create a large, successful consumer organization. The larger we become, the greater will be both our Contribution to our customers and distributors and to the vitality of our nation. We are truly following the universal law of life, which is:

YOU GET WHAT YOU GIVE!

"And, of course, we all know that we get out of life exactly what we put into it. We just need to quit forgetting it! And here we have the absolute, life-transforming value of working unitedly to enhance the individual empowerment of all of us together. Such an organization built around Contribution is a constant reminder of what works in life. It is a positive, creative, empowering structure within which to operate, a structure which brings us forth out of our vicious circle of survival.

"My good friends, have you ever noticed how well life works? The only time it doesn't is when we invalidate it, when we come from 'life doesn't work,' when we try to duplicate the 'crowd mentality'.

"History and economics have always proven the masses to be wrong. In the stock and commodity markets, the crowds always buy at the top and sell at the bottom. If you don't want your life to work, then follow the crowd; take the path of least resistance. On the other hand, if you want life to pay off on your terms, play full-out, play the Accelerated Game of Life. Dare to be different, dare to be a Winner."

The room erupted in a standing ovation for the man who was such a demonstration of his own words. Then as refreshments were served, George and Shirley Seeker were introduced to many of those present by both the Chins and their sponsor. They were impressed with the quality of these people and as they left nearly an hour later to drive home, Shirley sat very close to her husband, enjoying the warm feeling of confidence and well being engendered by their eventful evening.

CHAPTER FOURTEEN...

GETTING THE BALL ROLLING

Both George and Shirley Seeker again had difficulty getting to sleep that night. Even though it was late, the names of people who should go on their Special People List kept coming up. So when Harold Johnson arrived Monday evening, the list had grown to thirty-two. He shared their excitement as they reviewed the names of those who were the best candidates for their first three key players.

Their first step was to compare calendars to make up a schedule of open dates for possible Two-on-One appointments during the week.

Then Harold suggested, "Let's call these six to see

if one of them can either come over here tonight or if we can visit them.

"Isn't that pretty short notice?" George asked, a little surprised.

"Didn't The Winner tell you this is the Accelerated Game of Life? Can you think of anything more important for these people to be doing tonight than to enter a program that will enhance every area of their lives?"

They agreed and then George added, "I am glad you said that. I was getting a little nervous about what I would say when I call these people. Some we know well, others we don't, so I was trying to think of a way to explain to them how great this is. But really, all I need to do is let them know that I am excited about something terrific, and that I need to see them as soon as possible, like right NOW."

"Perfect George," Harold commented enthusiastically. "It took me a lot longer to catch onto creating a sense of urgency and curiosity. We really are taking charge of our lives. We are not begging anyone to join us. Instead, we are inviting them to embark on a fantastic journey. Of course, when you call, most will want to know what it is all about. Just reconfirm that it is the most encouraging thing you have ever seen and that they need to see it in its entirety like you did. You can mention the company name if you want, but other than that, leave the rest alone."

Out of the six calls, four were home. One could come that evening and one would be available Wednesday night. The other two made appointments early in

Getting the Ball Rolling

the next week. The Seekers were thrilled at how people responded to their enthusiasm and sense of urgency.

Harold acknowledged them, saying, "I want you to know that you did absolutely great. George, I can see why Irene says you are the best manager she has ever worked for."

Shirley spoke up, "Harold, it's now 6:30 and we have guests who will be here at 8:00. Let me put some dinner on the table and we can talk while we eat."

As they moved into the kitchen, Harold asked George to bring in his copy of the Distributor Manual. As the two men took seats at the dinette table, Harold said, "Turn to the back section to the work sheets. As I mentioned Friday night, we want to go over these agreements together to be sure we all have the same intention. George, will you read for us what you have written?"

As George reviewed his list of commitments, what he had chosen to stand for, and the levels of achievements toward his six month, twelve month, one year, six year and ten year goals, Harold added a number of helpful suggestions from his own experience and answered questions. Then he said, "I can't tell you how much sharing this process of working on your goals has meant to me. By the way, it is about eight o'clock, so let me coach you on your role with our guests. I will be covering the same material that you were given by The Winner, which is to help them identify what they would most like to be doing with their life and what it means to come from CONTRIBUTION instead of

SURVIVAL. Then, if the approach appeals to them, I will give the benefits of our distributorship like John Davis did for you at the breakfast meeting.

"Now, when they come, your role is to greet them and acknowledge them for their willingness to come on such short notice. Then introduce me in the very warmest way you can and support me with close attention and body language, but without saying a word.

"You see," Harold continued, "people usually trust their friends but they know them too well to believe that they could know more than they do about being really successful. In other words, although people tend to trust their friends, they usually do not respect them as financial or psychological geniuses. At the same time, they are more apt to respect a stranger who has been well recommended by a friend they trust. So with you as their friend and myself as the stranger, we have the perfect combination. This is called Two-on-One."

That evening, their friends were very much intrigued with the whole concept and dates were set for the lesson on the Ten Principles of Accelerated Winning and the goal setting session that the Seekers had enjoyed so much the Friday before.

As George and Shirley retired that night, they marveled at how fast their world had turned around. They could see that it was just the beginning of a much more fulfilling life.

CHAPTER FIFTEEN...

THE BIMONTHLY FORUM

The next week was also a great learning experience. The Seekers found how true it is that any Accelerated Game of Life magnifies and compresses the pleasure and the pain of learning new skills and expanding relationships. Two of their six friends were enthusiastically committed to becoming WINNERS. Two others were taking more time, while the other two, for various reasons, were not really interested. However, by the end of the week, one of their new recruits already had two people, and the other had one, so there was a great deal to celebrate.

In addition, all week they had been looking forward to Friday evening which was listed on their

The Greatest Home Based Business in the World

calendar as the Bimonthly Forum, Johnson's home for Potluck, 7:00.

Not only would the Seekers get to meet the Johnsons' other first-level people again, but Larry Guide, the one who had sponsored Irene and Lee Chin, would be there. This would be the Chin's first Forum, so Larry had volunteered to come and assist.

After the dinner, Harold Johnson opened the meeting by welcoming the group and acknowledging them all for preparing and bringing the delicious feast. The first item on the agenda was sharing the benefits derived from use of the company's products. Next on the agenda was recognition for what each couple had achieved in relation to their goals. Applause and cheers were frequent. At final count, after less than three weeks in the program, the Johnsons had fifteen in their organization, thanks to their fiends in the room. Lee Chin reminded him that he was now self-funded because his overrides would more than cover his monthly product costs. Everyone clapped in recognition of this significant milestone.

"The third item," Harold continued, "is for each of us to share our experiences of what is happening to us personally in working the business by answering three questions:

1. What experiences have I had which have increased my commitment?

2. What difficult experiences have tempted me to quit?

3. How has this business enabled me to make a difference in another person's life?

"Let's take number one first. I would like to lead off. Claudia and I have been in this business for less than a month. During that time we have had more incredible experiences than I think we have had in the last five years. One of the greatest experiences happened to us just ten days ago. We had accepted the ten-day challenge to get three people and had recruited two of you in a hurry. Then, for one reason or another, we hadn't gotten our third one yet. Our Team Managers, Lee and Irene Chin, asked us to attend the goal setting session with the Seekers, because they wanted us to get acquainted with them and see if we wanted them as one of our 'key players'.

"You know, I have never received so much support, acknowledgment and nurturing in my life. As I have gotten to know this great couple, working with them and the rest of you, I have never been so committed to any program, company, or project as I have this plan for a better life. I want to thank you all for making such an incredible contribution to my life."

There were cheers and an enthusiastic round of applause. Then each, as he or she felt inclined, shared experiences. As they got into the second question of relating some of their discouraging experiences, the group found themselves laughing until their sides hurt. The ones laughing the most were telling stories on themselves, seeing the humor in taking situations so seriously. They found how good it felt to laugh at disappointments.

However, several in the group asked for assistance or suggestions on particular situations which did not seem to be working. Some very helpful hints were shared and much appreciated.

The third question brought out some amazing stories about how they had benefited from this new way of being empowered. However, the most thrilling were those accounts of what was already happening to their friends as they were being brought into the Winning Program and finding a new lease on life.

At this point, Harold turned the meeting over to their guest, Larry Guide, who had also been participating in the sharing, particularly with examples of what insights he had received from some of the company's Advanced Seminars.

As Larry stood, he took a long look at the group with a big smile on his face, and said, "When I see what is happening to each of us, I am amazed at how quickly a better life is created from commitment, contribution and integrity.

"What we are finding, my friends, is that these Forums are a powerful element in our program. As you know, each of us will be in a meeting like this once a week. Every second week we will be meeting with our own Team Manager and each in-between week with our own key players. As you know, these meetings can be held in conjunction with breakfast, lunch or dinner, or just an informal session without refreshments. I prefer the dinner meetings, at least once a month, with each group. Be creative and do different things so that they stay exciting.

"The reason these Forums are so important is that they help us maintain integrity within our organizations. You know, the first of our Ten Principles is STRUCTURING. By your attendance here tonight, you are making a statement to your Team Manager that you are a committed player. You see, it is a necessity that, if we decide to no longer keep our commitments, we let our Team Manager know and not leave him guessing. We certainly have the right to change our minds, but there is a way to do it with integrity.

"By your own attendance at your Team Manager's Forum, you are setting the pace for your own first-level distributors. It is important for you to keep your commitments and prove it through Forum participation. It is a natural law, folks, that your integrity and your commitment will show up in your own organization.

"As you have observed tonight in the great job being done by Harold, the format of the meeting is:

1) acknowledging WINS that have accumulated since the last meeting,
2) group sharing on the three questions,
3) a discussion on one of the Ten Principles,
4) a report on the status of our groups,
5) then we plan the next two weeks.

"The Forum program maintains the integrity and commitment of your organization because you know, when you meet with your key people, that the following week they will be meeting with their key people. In this way we have eliminated the two greatest problems in networking, which are the lack of communication and follow up."

Larry paused and then asked, "Do you have any questions you would like discussed?"

The question was asked, "What do you do if one of your key players lives in another state?"

"That is a good question," Larry responded. "Let me encourage you to concentrate close to your home base at first. It might be easy to sponsor 'orphans' in far away places, but not easy to be their Team Manager until you have demonstrated success here. Until we are experienced enough and capable of giving them real support and management, these far away people have a very high probability of dying on the vine.

"The purpose of structuring your people's commitments is that you have a clear agreement as to what is required. Folks, it is very important to start your people out right. You will want to make it clear that each of your first three first-level positions are given on the basis of trust in the integrity of a real commitment to effectively work the business."

The Hundredth Monkey

"I don't know how many of you have heard the Hundredth Monkey Story, but I want to retell it to make an important point. As you have already found, when you tell most people about the difference between coming from Survival instead of Contribution, they look at you a little strange. It is such a basic concept and the masses are so caught up in Survival that Contribution is almost like a foreign language.

Well, just as there is a paradigm shift from straight retailing to networking, so will there be a gigantic shift from Survival to Contribution. I believe that the true spirit of network marketing can be the catalyst that brings this about. As you know, this is what our company is all about. But this story can show us that the paradigm shift to Contribution will not require a mass conversion of most of the people. All we need is something called a CRITICAL MASS. So let me review the story.

"Ken Keyes wrote a book called *The 100th Monkey* in which he recorded the findings of a scientific expedition. The expedition was a large one, sponsored by the National Geographic Society, and they witnessed what has been named the Critical Mass Theory. This phenomena is unexplainable by ordinary scientific methods, yet it works throughout life, and I believe that it is inevitable that it will help usher in the new era in compassion and service.

"In order to clarify the Critical Mass Theory, we'll take a look at how it was discovered. The time frame was 1952 to 1958 and the place was a number of islands off the coast of southern Japan. The report came from a group of scientists whose purpose was to observe and record the characteristics and habits of the local plant and animal life.

"The monkeys who inhabited the islands were of particular interest. The scientists gave them names and recorded their activities in a diary. The monkeys' main food source was sweet potatoes, which the scientists would scatter on the ground. The monkeys liked the taste of the raw potatoes, but found the dirt unpleasant.

"On the island of Koshima, a young female monkey named Imo found that she could solve the problem by washing her potatoes in a nearby stream. She taught this trick to her mother and her playmates, who also taught their mothers.

This cultural innovation was gradually picked up by various monkeys. During the six-year period, many of the Koshima monkeys learned to wash their sweet potatoes in order to make them more palatable.

"In the autumn of 1958 something startling took place - a breakthrough - a new era began. When the phenomena took place, the exact number of monkeys who had learned to wash their sweet potatoes was unknown. But one morning, when that number reached a certain point, let's say 100, it happened. By that evening almost every monkey in the tribe was washing its sweet potatoes.

"The added energy of this 100th monkey somehow created a quantum ideological breakthrough. Yet, the most surprising thing noticed by the scientists was that the habit of washing sweet potatoes suddenly and

The Bimonthly Forum

spontaneously jumped across the ocean. Colonies of monkeys on the other islands and even the mainland troops of monkeys began washing their sweet potatoes on that very same day.

"The only way the scientists could theorize as to what caused the phenomenon was by applying a theory of Quantum Mechanics called the Critical Mass Theory. This theory states that when a critical number achieve a certain awareness, this new awareness can be communicated from mind to mind. Although the exact number may vary, the 100th monkey phenomenon means that when a limited number of people know of a new way, a point is reached where only one more person needs to tune into the new awareness to cause it to reach almost everyone else.

"The group dynamics of extrasensory communication can be amplified to a powerfully effective level when the consciousness of the hundredth monkey is added. Your awareness is needed to usher in the new era in Contribution. You may be 'the hundredth' person. You may furnish the added consciousness energy necessary to create the image of networking as an industry based upon Contribution."

As Larry Guide told the story, most of those present had not heard the story and listened to the conclusion with some astonishment. After some interesting comments and questions, he continued.

"As I mentioned before, these Forums are a major part of our empowerment into Contribution. They are a weekly reminder that if we're going to play, we're going to play by the rules. Your Team Manager has the right to have evidence that you are really committed. Thank you for letting me share your first Forum session tonight."

The group gave Larry a strong round of acknowledgment. Then Harold Johnson asked each person to give a brief report of how he or she had achieved his or her goals of the last two weeks and what their next seventy-two hour and ten-day commitments were. He then renewed his own commitment, to be in touch with each one of them daily by phone, and asked for their commitments to do the same for their key players. He renewed his "$10 if I miss" pledge and got their agreements that they would accept the responsibility of enforcing it without mercy.

As the meeting ended, there were many pleased comments of how valuable the evening had been and how much the members truly appreciated each other.

As George and Shirley Seeker headed home, they had so much to talk about. They were impressed with their new friends at the Johnson's Forum Meeting, especially Harold and Claudia Johnson, themselves. They could hardly wait until they held their own Forum next week.

The Seekers third week was another period of learning, growing and accomplishments. Their three key players were on board and taking hold. George and Shirley conducted their first Forum session at their home. Lee and Irene Chin had come to give extra support and the first lesson.

The Bimonthly Forum

There was a special excitement anticipating their first Monthly Forum which was scheduled for the following evening.

In his talk, Lee explained the importance of all attending the Monthly Forum. Then he said, "The meeting begins at 7:59 sharp, and they don't mean 7:58 or 8:00. However, we want you there half an hour early, at 7:30, to participate in the preliminary Acknowledging Exercise."

George interrupted with a chuckle, "The what exercise?"

Lee smiled back and answered, "Which one of our Ten Principles is right smack in the middle? Can anyone tell me quickly?"

One of the group answered, "It's number 5, that would be NOURISHING."

"Right!" Lee exclaimed. "That means giving appreciation, compliments and attention to others, doesn't it? We all know how wonderful it is to receive nourishment, but how often do we forget to nourish others. If we want to change our habits, we must increase the <u>what</u> for change?"

"THE NECESSITY!" the group responded, smilingly shouting out to fill in the blank.

"Right!" Lee said in a praising voice. "So we precede the Monthly Forum Meeting with a half hour warm-up for all of us to get better acquainted, give each other attention and be very liberal with our compliments. We will all have name tags with our first names in big letters and we wear the tags high on our right shoulders. That's important."

"That's interesting, Lee," George added. "I usually wear my identification over my left breast pocket. Why high on the right shoulder?"

"Stand up here George, and I'll show you. You see," as their hands joined, "as we shake hands, my eyes naturally drop to your right hand so that I can make contact. Then my eyes move up from your right hand to your face. If I need to see your name and it is tucked down on your left side, I must make an obvious detour with my eyes. But when your name tag is on your right shoulder, I can see your name automatically as my eyes move up from your hand to your eyes."

George nodded his head in agreement.

"Incidentally, we will have a Greeter's Prize. A mystery person will have a special assignment to keep track of who is the twentieth person shaking his hand. Later in the program, that person will be given a special gift, so I would like to see the hands of those who want to 'come to practice' and choose to make a commitment to be there by 7:30." All but two hands went up. "Okay, that is fabulous. Shirley will you make a list of those who have made the agreement, and I would like to ask you to take charge of seeing that we keep that agreement."

"What do I do?" Shirley Seeker asked.

"Nothing unless one of us breaks our agreement. Then hold us to account. If I come late, I am to acknowledge to you that I have broken my agreement. If I do not show up at all, then you should contact me later.

"You see, friends, if we really care about each other and we have made a commitment of absolute integrity, we want to assist each other in being responsible for agreements. True integrity creates a positive energy in the Universe, and an absence of it works in reverse. Acknowledging a broken agreement at least turns the energy positive again.

"If no one calls us on our broken agreements, we are encouraged to continue, just by default. Our purpose is not to accuse or blame, it is to help the person acknowledge that he did break his agreement.

"I am not trying to be metaphysical, folks. It is just amazing what begins to happen in our lives when we start becoming responsible about what we say we are going to get done. Our Winning Program is about the power to make up our mind and see what is necessary to make something happen.

As for next Tuesday night, I will see you all, except for those two, at 7:30, right?"

There was a resounding, enthusiastic response, "RIGHT!"

The Greatest Home Based Business in the World

I never think of the future. It comes soon enough.

Albert Einstein

CHAPTER SIXTEEN...

THE MONTHLY FORUM

Tuesday night there was a big crowd by 7:30. Lee was absolutely right about the powerful nourishing effect of the socializing period. Everyone kept involved, cheerfully, enthusiastically and joyfully responding to the compliments thrown their way.

The organization committee had arranged for the meeting room, the registration group handled "sign in" and name tags, the decorations committee had arranged product displays, banners and several posters. Another group was selling raffle tickets, the committee's way of raising money to pay for the room. Tickets were one for $1.00, ten for $5.00 and thirty tickets for $10.00. For the raffle, there were some special prizes provided by vendors, plus some marketing and training aids, books, audio cassettes and video tapes. The room was filled with nearly three hundred happy, talkative people by the time the regular meeting was to start.

John Davis, who had given the Coffee Shop orientation that George had attended, called the meeting to order at 7:59. As everyone quieted down, John requested, "Would all of those who are guests here tonight please stand so we can recognize you."

About forty people stood to a warm welcome of applause.

As the guests sat down, he asked, "Now would all of those who are committed to making a CONTRIBUTION through our business stand. Let's really acknowledge each other."

The room erupted again into applause as all but a few of the guests stood. "Now please remain standing if you have personally sponsored at least your three key players who, are committed to WINNING."

Nearly half remained standing, receiving their acknowledgment. "Will all of those who have at least nine Associates on their second-level please remain standing." All but fifty-six took their seats while everyone clapped, including those standing. "Now we are getting tougher. Will those of you who have at least one Qualified Team remain standing." Twenty-two remained on their feet and were acknowledge with gusto.

"Now, will those who are Team Managers, having three Qualified Teams, remain standing and come to the front." The five remaining were asked to take several minutes to tell about how their experiences were enabling them to stay in COMMITMENT. The talks were a mixture of dramatic stories and humorous incidents which held everyone spellbound.

The next part of the program had to do with additional recognition awards. The first was given to those who had sponsored three people since the last Monthly Forum. As the Seekers stood, they noticed a number of friends, such as Harold and Claudia Johnson and their own three first-level distributors. They all sent big smiles of mutual acknowledgment between them.

Also, there was special recognition for those Associates who were at their first Monthly Forum. George and Shirley were proud to again stand and be recognized along with nearly forty others. As they stood to the applause, Davis asked those who had already earned $500 or more to remain standing. Half of the group stayed on their feet, to the cheers of the audience. The Seekers and the Johnsons were among them. As they sat down, Shirley whispered to her husband, "These people find all kinds of ways to have fun, don't they?" George agreed.

Next came the raffle. It was handled quickly and with precision. Each winner remained up front to be acknowledged collectively. Several short announcements were made. Finally, The Winner was introduced. He had been a very popular participant in the warm-up, socializing session. Now everyone was waiting with keen anticipation for him to introduce the speaker of the evening, his friend who had introduced him to our company.

"Ladies and gentlemen," The Winner began in a strong, forceful voice, "we all are finding out what it is to come from CONTRIBUTION. I am here tonight because a good friend hit me over the head with a ten ton wake-up call, and that friend is here tonight. To put it mildly, in this special way, my wife and I owe him our lives.

As most of you know, my wife and I have always been deeply spiritual, but this new life has shown us that we were just touching the tip of the Infinite iceberg. He woke us up so that we could take back the deeper, richer part of our lives that we had unknowingly lost over the years. May I warmly introduce this great man to you, Steve Teacher."

Immediately, out of their great respect for what Steve had, indirectly, brought into all their lives, the entire room rose for a standing ovation. Gradually, as the acknowledgment ended and all sat down, Steve began to speak.

"I want to thank all of you for your wonderful welcome. The Winner has told me so much about you. What you all have started here is going to have an impact on your city which none of us can even begin to comprehend. I want you to know that I am truly humbled and grateful to have been able to play a small part. As you know, our theme, WINNING, is based upon helping each of us discover our own magnificence. We transform our lives by experiencing the greatness of where our gift of Life is coming from, rather than having an attachment to how it's going to turn out. That is why the Positive Expressions we use are so powerful.

"People who make a positive impact in the world are not much different from others. They just develop certain characteristics which enable them to be effective. These aptitudes are such things as staying on purpose, being committed, being trustworthy and trusting others. I have discovered that INTEGRITY is not another position to play in the game of life, IT IS THE GAME.

"I would like to share an experience that happened to a very dear friend of mine. Her name is Susan Bradford. When Susan came into her kitchen one very windy morning to make breakfast for herself and her three-year-old daughter, Amanda, she found the child lying semiconscious on the kitchen floor. Amanda had been awakened by a severe storm and, unknown to her mother, had come to the kitchen to play. An open, empty pill bottle laying beside the little girl told the rest of the story.

"Susan quickly read the label on the bottle, which said that death from over-dosage could occur within half an hour after loss of consciousness. Having no pockets in her night gown, Susan clutched the empty bottle in her hand, picked up Amanda and ran to the garage to get the car.

"A tree had fallen during the storm, blocking the driveway. She dashed back to the house to call a neighbor. The phone was dead, the line having been severed by the falling tree.

"Susan grabbed her child and ran across a field to a nearby freeway. Although clothed in her nightgown, with her hair still in curlers, she was unconcerned about either the cold wind or her appearance. She climbed over the fence, crossed to the center of the freeway, set Amanda down on the median strip and stepped into the fast lane to wave down a car. She got a ride immediately. Amanda was at the nearest hospital emergency room within a few minutes.

"Later, when her friends asked her what she would have done if nobody had stopped to help her, Susan said, 'I'd have laid down on the freeway or whatever it took until somebody did stop.' She added, 'I saw myself in the hospital emergency room with Amanda the moment I read the label. It never occurred to me that I wouldn't make it. I didn't think about anything else but getting there. I just did whatever I had to do until that's where I was.'

"Friends, commitment means just one thing. It means the mind has locked in on an INTENTION, a decision. Only a clear, decisive intention gives you that all consuming determination and burning desire. When we see clearly what we would like to be that we are not, what we would like to be doing that we are not, and what we would like to have which we do not, we stop procrastinating and start going towards those goals.

"Let me ask you a serious question. How many books on leadership would you have to read for it to have an impact on your ability to lead? How many success stories would you have to hear for it to have an impact on your ability to be a success? Well, I say that there won't be much of an impact, no matter how many you read or hear!

"To improve your ability, you must play the game. You see, the reason the 'how tos', the techniques, the rituals don't work is because it's not the understanding but <u>the doing</u> which produces results. You already know everything you need to know, you already have everything you need to have, you can do everything you need to do, and you are everything you need to be in order to experience success. You don't need someone else's style or technique. You need only to be YOU.

"The secret is to play - to play full-out! You have the ability to be human and to contribute to other humans. Your natural, 'God given' talents need merely to be channeled in the right direction, and that's the purpose of our WINNING PROGRAM.

"When you play the game according to the Ten Scientific Principles, you play with power. Your power comes as a result of defined intentions, pursued committedly. Your natural abilities are focused on specific results. You know exactly what to do and when to do it -- no guessing -- no going off on tangents -- no spinning your wheels.

"It was a great experience for me when I saw clearly how simple life really is -- just keep my agreements and get the job done. That's why this business is such an incredible vehicle. We have a saying which I would like to repeat.

'The only way to stay in the realm of contribution is to sponsor others into it.'

"That is the incredible business we are in, inviting others into the Accelerated Game of Life. Yes, folks, we can get everything in life we really want if we will help enough other people get what they want. And what everyone really wants the most, whether they are conscious of it or not, is what we call unconditional love, affection, appreciation and devotion.

"How can we get all of the love we want? Simple! By helping other people get all the unconditional love they want? I am not talking about sympathy or agreement. I am talking about valuing, appreciating and honoring the miracle of life which is in every living thing, especially every human being.

"The answer is that love, in spite of the common assumption of the masses, is never experienced as it comes toward us. It is only experienced as it flows from within outward. If we are not feeling love, we are not loving. If we are not feeling support, we are not supporting. When we are experiencing love, it is something WE ARE DOING.

"That is why this business enables all of us to be committed to a more complete life of FULFILLMENT, and it provides us the opportunity to inspire others to become committed to it as well. It is easy when we come from commitment, contribution, and integrity. It doesn't work that well any other way. When people go through the motions without a powerful aim, it is real exhausting work. However, when we work with a clear, exciting intention, it is play. It is like magic in your life. So dust off your magic wand and go for it full-out! Share the magic!"

In conclusion, Steve Teacher acknowledged the great contribution all in the room had made to him that night. Then he said, "I want to leave you with a poem that has meant a great deal to me over the last few months. It has to do with the way we pretend to care and do not care, the way we pretend to ask and do not ask, the way we pretend to listen and do not listen. The subject of the poem is prayer, but it applies to all of our relationships, especially in our families -- even in that inner relationship with ourselves."

At that point, Steve became quiet as he looked intently at the audience. Then, starting with a carefree voice, he said:

"I knelt to pray when day was done,
And prayed, Oh Lord, bless everyone.
Lift from the saddened heart the pain
And let the sick be well again."

With a smile, he paused briefly, looking up with a satisfied look on his face, then continued.

"Then I arose another day,
And carelessly went on my way.
All day long I did not try
To wipe the tear from any eye.
I did not even go to see
The sick man just next door to me."

Steve Teacher paused while his words seemed to hang in the air. Then in a much deeper voice, speaking more slowly, he continued.

"Then again when day was done,
I prayed, Oh Lord, bless everyone!
And as I prayed, into my ear,
There came a voice that whispered clear.
'Pause now my son, before you pray.
Whom have you tried to bless today.
God's sweetest blessings always flow
By hands that serve him here below.'"

After a short pause, Steve whispered distinctly into the microphone,

"And then I hung my head and cried.
'Forgive me, God, I have not tried.
Let me but live another day,
And I will Live the way I pray.'"

As he left the stand, the appreciative audience gave him another standing ovation. It had been a real inspiration to see the man who had touched just one, yet made such a difference in all their lives.

As George and Shirley Seeker were driving home that evening, they marveled at what had happened to them in less than a month and commented about the fact that Steve Teacher, just like The Winner, was another walking demonstration of the fact that the best is yet to come.

CHAPTER SEVENTEEN...

CONCLUSION

This story is an allegory, of course, but what was happening to George and Shirley Seeker and their many new friends can and should be repeated hundreds of thousands of times. The Ten Principles of Winning can be cooperatively and systematically incorporated into your own life and the lives of those in your organization, whether those above you do so or not.

That is what is so beautiful about building your own networking business. You are the president and creator of your business organization. At the same time, you are "vice-president" in your Team Manager's business, and genuine leadership can go up just as easily as it can go down.

The Greatest Home Based Business in the World

So how does one proceed? This book is only one step in launching this exciting, revolutionary approach to a QUALITY LIFE. However, the greatest innovations and ideas will be created by YOU and then proven in the field.

Start with this base, then adapt and create what works for you and your people.

The FIRST STEP is to make a decision, a personal, all-out commitment to Life, Empowerment and Fulfillment, by Accelerating the Game of Life. Determine your primary purpose and write it down. Make your "Be - Do - Have - Contribute" goals for the next six months, twelve months, three years, six years and ten years. Sign your agreements and keep them!

The SECOND STEP is to duplicate your commitment by getting agreement from those who also want to commit to being WINNERS by:

1. Selecting the best people you can.

2. Planning a careful strategy for reaching them, using a Two-on-One approach, if you can. Your first purpose is to prioritize your list to see which of your friends are really interested in a better life.

3. As new people come aboard, get agreements and commitments from them to do what you have done.

STEP THREE is to help form a local support system in your area, if one does not exist. Volunteer to help on the committees since they are designed to

Conclusion

involve as many people as possible. Everyone needs a part. Spread the work so it does not become a distraction from the primary task of building a personal business.

I believe we create lucky breaks in life, but more important, we must ask ourselves whether we are really ready to commit, to "burn-the-bridges," to be like the mother who knew she was going to get to that emergency room with her dying little girl? Of course there are going to be obstacles and disappointments. Sure we are not going to have our way as often as we would like. Yes, people will misunderstand us and not always give us their support. These things can hurt. They can hurt a lot. But are the victories that we experience worth it? Yes, indeed -- you can bet your bottom dollar!

My greatest lessons have come from athletics, where the competition is so intense, and where I've had to run full-out. Personally, I'm convinced that the phrase "no gain without pain" has merit. Is it worth the pain? Is it worth the trauma, the exhaustion, the training, the commitment?

Let me just say this. It never "hurts so much as it feels good" to cross the finish line in FIRST PLACE! It never "hurts so much as it feels good" to feel the tape break across your chest, experiencing the thrill of thousands of people rising to their feet and applauding a great race! It never "hurts so much as it feels good" to feel the inner excitement of standing on top of the victory stand and having a first place medal placed

The Greatest Home Based Business in the World

around your neck. So no matter how great the pain and the price, it is nothing when compared to the thrill, the joy, the inner glow and satisfaction that come from WINNING.

We can't all be the one who breaks the tape, but we can all WIN -- because we gave it our all.

As our Winning Program evolves, we will acquire the keys for unlocking, more completely, the precious gift of unconditional love. It is then that we can experience each other as members of one infinite family, made up of great, incredible beings, participating as invited guests at a fascinating party called LIFE, on a beautiful estate called EARTH.

I congratulate the people who are building their own home based direct selling businesses. I encourage you to join them in their effort to generate a QUALITY LIFE through WINNING.

Part Three...
Epilogue

In this section, we look at some of the basics of starting your own business that many people overlook.

Home based businesses are not for everyone. This candid look at some "pros & cons" may help you determine the type of business that's right for you.

CHAPTER EIGHTEEN...

STARTING YOUR OWN BUSINESS!

Personally, I can't imagine any occupational opportunity offering as much satisfaction and fulfillment as successfully running your own business. I'm not referring to a business that runs you, but an ideal business which you learned about in Chapter One.

Owning your own ideal business truly allows you to experience health, wealth, and fulfillment. For direct sales to be your ideal business, you must create space in your life and mind for it to be that. You must think of it, treat it, and respect it as a business.

The Greatest Home Based Business in the World

YOUR OWN NETWORK

If you see direct sales as nothing more than an opportunity to be a sales person for some company, you're missing the boat. As such, you'll always be at the mercy of that company and their reputation. Instead of being just a sales person and being totally dependent upon company XYZ, set up your own independent network through which to market the products and/or services of whatever company you choose to represent.

I'm not saying start a manufacturing company. Lord knows you don't want those headaches. Besides, the sales and marketing of products and services can be the most lucrative part of the business world.

There are so many facets to starting and owning a business, that most everyone makes a series of mistakes in the process. The goal of this Chapter is twofold:

First, I want to help raise your consciousness to that of a business owner. It seems that in the world of direct sales, only a small percentage of people actually treat it as a business.

Secondly, I hope that you can learn from my mistakes.

The following ideas can make a big difference in how you experience business ownership.

STATEMENT OF PURPOSE

The very foundation of any business has got to be a statement of purpose!

> My puppose is to help people discover their magnifience and potential and to empower them to live quality lives, and become the best that they can be!

Why do you want a business, and what do you want to achieve? This step is critical.

Once your purpose is clear, you can write a business plan involving the "nuts and bolts," so you won't have to "fly by the seat of your pants".

A casual approach is appropriate on some osions, but not here! Your business plan could include some of the following:

IMAGE: Company Name, Literature, etc.

PERMITS AND FILINGS: Corporation, Sole Proprietorship, Partnership, etc.

ACCOUNTING: Bank Account, Bookkeeping, Records, etc.

OVERHEAD: Rent, Equipment, Telephone & Fax Lines, Advertising, etc.

MANAGEMENT: Commitment, Leadership, Problem Solving, Acknowledgment, etc.

The Greatest Home Based Business in the World

Let's examine each of these individually:

IMAGE

Your image starts with your company name. The phrase, "You never get a second chance to make a first impression," is true about company names.

You may want to name the company after yourself, but some people feel like it's less professional to use their personal name, so they pick a name like, "The Pacesetters".

Upon settling on a name, you need to present a stable, professional image, graphically. If possible, have an artist design your letterhead, envelope and business card. The money spent here is an investment. These tools will last throughout your business career.

PERMITS AND FILINGS

In order to open a bank account in your company name, your ownership needs to be filed of public record. Your state or county government may require that you file a dba (doing business as) or Fictitious Business Name. As long as the name you have chosen is available, you can file it as your Fictitious Name.

Only you and/or your tax advisor could determine if you would benefit by setting up a privately owned corporation. Rarely is it advantageous for an individual to start out in business by incorporating. If you wish to incorporate in your state, the necessary filings are probably done with your Secretary of State. Many people, today, are doing business through Limited Partnerships, Business Trusts and Limited Liability Companies.

ACCOUNTING

When you own a business, especially one that's home based, you are blessed with a multitude of tax deductions which you would not otherwise have. The key to taking advantage of them is record keeping.

We pay all business bills out of our business checking account and charge all business travel, lodging, and meals to credit cards. Receipts for deductible items paid for with cash go into a "petty cash file." At the end of each month, these receipts are totaled, and a business check is written to "cash," which replenishes our petty cash box and creates a single checkbook entry for a large number of miscellaneous items.

You may want to set up hanging files in your desk and organize records similar to the following:

Accounts Payable, Accounts Paid, Advertising, Business Promotion, Cash Receipts, Equipment, Home Office, Insurance, Inventory, Legal & Professional, Miscellaneous, Petty Cash, Postage & Printing, Shipping, Stationary, Supplies, Taxes, Telephone & Utilities, etc.

In order to make the most out of what you have, you need to do three things: organize, organize, and organize.

OVERHEAD

The main thing that you need to know about overhead is to avoid it like the plague. Excessive overhead has destroyed more businesses than all of the other factors combined. Every dollar increase in monthly overhead represents another dollar of profit that must be earned each month just to break even. To be sure, stress and overhead are interconnected. If you want to keep your stress low and your chances of success high, avoid unnecessary overhead. Strive to maintain high image with low overhead. An ideal business is one in which this combination is possible.

MANAGEMENT

In many cases, managing your own business boils down to managing yourself. Unless your business activities take precedence over hobbies, recreation, and just plain laziness, you probably won't do well as a business owner. Starting a business and nurturing it to a source of financial independence requires commitment, dedication and long hours. Most successful business owners work more than forty hours per week, especially during the first few years.

LEADERSHIP

Since direct sales / networking is a people business, success is directly related to the development of leadership skills.

Lawrence Miller, in his book titled *The American Spirit,* makes a significant distinction between being a manager and a leader. He states that most executives in America today are managers, but not leaders. While managers are adept at the technical and mechanical aspects of business, leaders are adept in the area of human relations. "Leaders are those rare individuals who inspire a sense of purpose, a sense of belonging, a sense of loyalty."

Mr. Miller says that there is very little loyalty in corporate America today because most corporate officers have either lost their sense of purpose, or are unable to inspire their key executives to have a sense of purpose.

So, do you have a noble purpose for being in business? Can you communicate that sense of purpose to your organization in such a way that they get a true experience of it? You can if you choose to! As you help meet the needs which exist in this area of business, your own needs will be met as well.

PROBLEM SOLVING

What about problems? You're not going to have any, right? You're going to start a business and live happily ever after! Well guess what! Life is about problems, and business ownership is about even more problems. If you think you've got problems now, you haven't seen nothin' yet!

And that's great. Problems are the stuff that personal growth and personal satisfaction are made out of. Problem solving is one of the most exciting aspects of life, and as long as you're satisfactorily solving them, "the more the merrier."

When a problem arises, our natural tendency is to bury our head in the sand, or to ignore it and maybe it will go away.

No matter what the problem, it should be confronted head on, with both eyes open, with compassion and total honesty. Most business and relationship problems can be resolved quickly, if you're willing to accept responsibility for them and their solution.

ACKNOWLEDGMENT

In business, people are the greatest asset. We must acknowledge this fact and never lose sight of it. People make the world go around! Don't let anything get in the way of your acknowledging their magnificence and their contribution to your success.

CHAPTER NINETEEN...

BUSINESS OWNERSHIP

People come to the United States, from all over the world, because its the land of opportunity! Ours is a country where anyone can create wealth through business ownership and skilled investing. All you have to do is take some risk and work real hard.

More people are becoming millionaires in the United States now, than at any time during recorded history. It's the age of the entrepreneur, the age of the small business person. Entrepreneurs have been around since the beginning of time, and their cycle of prominence is here.

The Greatest Home Based Business in the World

In the 1950's, we went through the "Sputnik Craze," the high-tech, scientific approach to business. Big was the only way! Businesses had to be run by computers and research studies! We became mathematical and mechanical. The same strategies that caused us to dominate the market place, eventually caused us to lose that dominance. Why? Because businesses are people, and you have to run your business according to people, not statistics.

No matter what your background or age, if you can discover a market that is not being taking care of, you can become very successful. In actuality, most successful businesses are not original ideas. They are an adaptation of an existing business. Someone recognizes that a particular need is not being met, and they step in. Apple Computer is a prime example.

Computers had been around for a long time, and IBM dominated the market. Steven Jobs discovered the need for inexpensive, personal computers and created an empire.

What you want to do is recognize that you have just as much ability and potential business success as anyone in the universe. You just need to learn the rules and strategies of business ownership.

The first step is to develop a healthy attitude toward risk and reward. We're all familiar with the phrase, "no pain - no gain," and we need to be just as familiar with "no risk - no reward"! Instead of seeking intelligent risk-taking opportunities through business ownership and skilled investing, most people look

Business Ownership

for safety, security, and guarantees. The guarantee seeker ends up frustrated and unachieved.

Of course you may fail in business. Most people do! The great thing about it is, you can try again. Personally, I have failed more often than not, but my successes have generated far more than my failures have cost. I have learned to cut my losses short and let my profits run.

Most businesses do not fail, however, for the reasons you have been told. Most businesses fail because the operators are not aware of the trends and do not know the rules of business management.

If you don't currently own a business, start thinking, speaking, and planning to do so. Wouldn't you rather spend more time "behind the cash register" and less time in front of it?

Wouldn't you like to own the dry cleaners, the pharmacy, the grocery store, the gas station, the McDonald's, etc.? Wouldn't you like to own them all? Somebody does! You've got to start thinking, "I want to own businesses."

All businesses are based on the concept of "make a little from a lot." Why does McDonald's sell their hamburgers between $2.00 and $4.00, instead of between $5.00 and $7.00? Because they have determined the optimum price at which they can sell the largest number of hamburgers.

All manufacturing companies are based on the same concept - volume - make a little from a lot. Yet,

The Greatest Home Based Business in the World

most small businesses don't do it. Most small businesses try to make a lot from a little, and it doesn't work.

When the first digital watches came out years ago, how much did they cost? $200 - $300 - $400? How much do they cost now? $10.95? Yet the manufacturers are making more money now, because they're making a little from a lot. This is a major business concept to keep in mind!

You can go into business as a start up, a franchise, or by purchasing an established business. Let's look at the basic rules for each.

START UPS:

The cardinal rule for a start up is "avoid fixed overhead". The normal temptation for a person starting their first business is to immediately go out and rent a store, fixtures, furniture, etc. It's so exciting! The problem is, at this point, it's an experimental business. If you use up your capital, and the business doesn't work out, you're still stuck with the rent, utilities, furniture, etc. Keep your fixed overhead to an absolute minimum. Work out of your home, or garage, forever if you can, and at least until the business is established and profitable.

My first business was in my apartment. My office was a desk in the bedroom. Nobody knew the difference. The person on the other end of the phone could care less. I was Mr. Ward, calling from my Executive Suite.

Business Ownership

That first business didn't last, and I wasn't stuck with a lot of overhead.

FRANCHISES:

If you're not interested in being creative and starting something original, you may want to look at a franchise. If so, I have a warning that you'll want to make note of. Franchises are "military organizations". You'd better be the disciplined type. This factor isn't either good or bad, but the thing to know is that you'll be required to run it the way they want you to, not the way you want to. It's a turnkey operation.

If you are a mover and a shaker, and a creator, you will be better off not getting involved in a franchise. If you like discipline, rules, and order, a franchise may be perfect for you. It's not good or bad, but is certainly a factor to be aware of.

Another rule is to avoid the high priced franchises. Look for a new, lower priced one. The franchise fees will be much less. The capital requirement will be much less, and they may even finance you.

ESTABLISHED BUSINESSES:

There are a lot of businesses for sale, and you can buy one with no money down, if you are skilled and patient. A rule to keep in mind here is to buy an established business that is profitable. You will pay a little more for a winner, but don't even consider buying a looser! You will be tempted to say, "I can turn it around." If it's your first experience out, don't try.

Wait until you are experienced at running a business before trying to rescue one that's failing. Look for a balance sheet and income statement that are positive rather than negative.

STEPS TO SUCCESS

If you want to own a business, you'd better be practical. You can't live in a fairy tale world. Business owners don't show up at 10:00 AM, go to lunch at noon, come back at 3:00 PM, check on the employees and go play golf at 4:30 PM.

Most new business owners work twice as long as their employees. If you own a business, you are the last one paid. You take all the risk. You have to manage people, creditors, bankers, etc.

It's not a glamorous activity, but you do it because the potential rewards are great. Business ownership requires total dedication!

The keys to a successful business are as follows:

1. You must have a goal to be successful. Business success is 95% attitude, dedication and hard work.

2. You must provide total customer satisfaction, even when it hurts.

Customers are your source of revenue. You, and your employees, must treat them like special people. And they are. They're your customers.

3. You must develop a unique selling benefit, a reason why people will want to buy from you instead of your competition.

Business Ownership

For example, you might establish a return policy that will allow your customers to return any purchase, no questions asked. This would give you a market edge on the competition because your customers could take their purchases home with confidence. You've eliminated, or reversed, the risk in doing business with you.

Never operate a "me too" business. If you're a carpenter, stop doing what all the other carpenters are doing. Do something different, whatever it takes. If you provide a service, develop a way to provide more service at less cost than your competitors. Always offer something unique.

As an employee, you can apply the same strategy. You're going to be paid according to your uniqueness.

If you don't make yourself unique, you're not creating a demand for yourself. Therefore, you will not be uniquely rewarded.

4. You must have excellent financial controls.

Spend a little time and money to learn about balance sheets and income statements. Rather than just looking at them, know how to read and understand them. They are specific financial tools that you must learn to work with. They tell you where your income is coming from, what your expenses are, whether your income is keeping pace with, or exceeding, your expenses, and so on.

5. Your business should have unlimited growth potential.

Don't limit your thinking. Through the use of duplication and leverage, you can own multiple businesses. Start or buy the first one, run it, learn it, develop it, hire someone to take your place and then start another, and so on. Repeat the process ten times and have 10 managers running 10 businesses for you. If you own just one, you may never achieve the financial success you desire and deserve. Most of the wealthy franchise owners have 10 or more. Shouldn't we copy them?

Whatever your business, duplication can offer unlimited growth potential.

ADDITIONAL STRATEGIES

As a business owner, it's your responsibility to create a customer orientated, fun place to work. The average business owner spends more time at work than at home. Running your business should be pleasurable, not painful. If you're the head of the business, and you're walking around grumbling and upset, and your employees are doing likewise, who's fault is it?

As an employee, will you ever experience personal satisfaction, if your attention is focused on complaining? If you work with the attitude, "I'm going to make this a fun place to work," you'll be in the front office in no time.

On the way to work, take a few minutes to ask yourself, "What can I do today to make this a better business, to improve it?" You will be amazed at the results.

Encourage open communication with customers

and employees. They are your greatest assets. By communicating openly with your employees and customers, you'll soon discover who knows how to run your business the best. It's not you! It's your employees and customers. Every day, they will give you the secrets which will guarantee your success, if you'll only listen.

If you want your employees to do something, lead them - don't command them! If you want your employees to be early birds, you've got to be the earliest bird. If you want them to work late, you can't leave early. If you want them to be enrolled in your project body, mind, and spirit, you must work side by side with them.

Read at least a half hour per day. Since knowledge is doubling every five years, the person who does not read is quickly becoming illiterate. Train yourself to read every day. Pick a specific time and place and stick with it. For most people, the best time is in the morning, when their mind is fresh. Late night is the worst time, since your body and mind are tired. The man who taught me this strategy leaves his house thirty minutes early, goes to a restaurant, and has a cup of coffee while he reads.

Another daily habit to develop is to listen to motivational and instructional tapes. Most of you have a cassette tape player in your car. What do you listen to? What do most people listen to? Songs and news broadcasts about murders, muggings, robberies, etc. How can they make you a positive person? No wonder you show up at work wanting to attack someone!

On the other hand, listening to positive tapes provides you with a cheerleading session in the morning. You'll know that great things are going to happen to you, that you're in control of your life, and that you're on the road to health, wealth, and fulfillment. When you show up for work, after a cheerleading session, you'll be smiling and feeling good, the people you meet will be smiling and feeling good, and what does it cost you? Nothing! Yet it will cost you not to do it. So listen to positive tapes on the way to work and encourage your employees to do the same.

Encourage your employees to experiment. Eliminate phrases like, "We don't do things like that around here." or "It's always been done this way." If your employees come to you with an idea, listen. If you'll trust them, they will produce much more value.

If you have financial backers, develop strong and honest communications with them. Always provide them with financial statements on a timely basis. Keep them properly informed, especially when you're in trouble. Don't wait until it becomes a catastrophe. Then, you not only have an irate backer, but you have one that doesn't trust you.

Finally, always build from within your company. Try to promote employees upward. Never go outside to fill a position, if it can be filled from within. If your employees know that they will not be overlooked for

Business Ownership

promotion, they'll feel more secure and be better employees.

As an employer, you have the responsibility to lead, motivate, and direct. As an employee, you have the same responsibilities, to lead, motivate and direct the customers. All businesses require customers. The customer is King, or Queen. When the King or Queen walks in, you don't abuse them - you love them, you nurture them. How often do you experience being treated well in a retail shop, and when it happens to you, isn't it a major event?

Do you want to own a business? How many cash registers do you want to own? As many as you can? In order to do it, you've got to practice the basic, proven philosophies.

> Without friends no one would choose to live, though he had all other goods.
>
> *Aristotle*

About the Author

Randy Ward, by the age of 35, had experienced success in a variety of areas. He worked his way through college as a top ten salesman for the Southwestern Publishing Company of Nashville. During college, he became a private pilot and currently holds a commercial pilot's certificate with multi-engine and instrument ratings.

Randy's first business venture beyond college was to write more than three million dollars worth of life insurance in two years. His rapid advancement toward financial independence began when he became a real estate broker and started his own company in 1976. Between 1976 and 1980, he bought, sold and constructed dozens of houses and developed over 2,000 acres of raw land into homesites.

In 1980, Randy became an oil producer and drilled 21 wells before entering the direct sales field in 1983. His first six month's group volume exceeded a million dollars.

Randy's diversified past has convinced him that the most rewarding way to achieve financial independence is through owning a home based business. He believes that skilled investing and business ownership are the only ways to create wealth.

Having founded and operated several successful businesses, he has come to realize that a home based, direct sales business offers unlimited potential with absolute freedom. It can be started on a shoestring, requires few, if any, employees, very little, if any, inventory and only basic accounting. Yet, direct selling offers the greatest of rewards, because it is a people business.

Randy calls direct sales "the Accelerated Game of Life" because it speeds up the process of personal growth and is a very direct path to friends, self-expression, wealth, travel and making a difference. He sees direct sales as a game, you as a player and coach, and his book, ***Winning the Greatest Game of All,*** as your guide. His book defines the game, explains the rules, tells you what to expect, outlines a proven game plan, and gives you a scoreboard with which to monitor your progress.

Randy considers direct sales as a vehicle through which lives can be transformed, a vehicle through which we can make a great and powerful contribution to others. Read **Winning the Greatest Game of All,** and you will be able to make a quality decision as to whether you want to play or merely be a spectator in "the Accelerated Game of Life". And if you decide to play, you will do so with focus and commitment, you will play full-out, and you will make a difference. In the process, you will help usher in what Randy calls "the new era in sales and marketing".

Currently, Randy is a "leading edge" Professional Speaker, sales trainer and consultant. He designs marketing plans and business strategies for companies. He has produced a variety of books and cassette tape series. Randy's most popular talk and workshop is called **"What Makes the Difference?".** It's about why some people produce a lot of results in life and most people don't. It is available on audio and video cassettes.

SPONSORING RANDY WARD

"The Voice that Makes a Difference"

For only $10, ***Making a Difference Seminars*** will send you a complete Introduction Packet that includes a 20-minute promotional video, a product catalog and information about our proven training systems. We will also include a list of training events and terms on how you can personally sponsor Randy Ward in your city.

Randy conducts a variety of exciting three-hour seminars and all-day workshops that will quickly and profitably accelerate your organization's growth!

For any additional information about ***Making a Difference Seminars,*** please feel free to contact us at:

Making a Difference Seminars
333 American Way, Jennings, OK 74038
(918) 757-2235, fax 757-2212
800-324-2266 (orders only)

Books & Tapes by Randy Ward

Featuring the *What Makes the Difference?* Seminar
and the *Making a Difference* Library

What Makes the Difference (3 audio cassettes)	$29.95
What Makes the Difference (video)	19.95
What Makes the Difference (paperback)	14.95
Selling - Recruiting - Managing (paperback/audio)	14.95
The Bulletproof Estate (paperback)	14.95
Winning the Greatest Game of All (paperback/audio)	12.95
Tapping the Source (paperback/audio)	12.95
The Greatest Home Based Business in the World	12.95
How to have Power with People (paperback/audio)	12.95
"Making a Difference" Library (SAVE $95)	125.00

Making a Difference Seminars
333 American Way, Jennings, OK 74038
(918) 757-2235, fax 757-2212
800-324-2266 (orders only)

"People don't CARE about what you have to say, until they know how much you CARE."

Books & Tapes by Randy Ward

Featuring the *What Makes the Difference?* Seminar
and the *Making a Difference* Library

What Makes the Difference (3 audio cassettes)	$29.95
What Makes the Difference (video)	19.95
What Makes the Difference (paperback)	14.95
Selling - Recruiting - Managing (paperback/audio)	14.95
The Bulletproof Estate (paperback)	14.95
Winning the Greatest Game of All (paperback/audio)	12.95
Tapping the Source (paperback/audio)	12.95
The Greatest Home Based Business in the World	12.95
How to have Power with People (paperback/audio)	12.95
"Making a Difference" Library (SAVE $95)	125.00

Making a Difference Seminars
333 American Way, Jennings, OK 74038
(918) 757-2235, fax 757-2212
800-324-2266 (orders only)

"A short pencil is better than a long memory."

Larry Adebesin